Succeed in
English

Published by
Arcturus Publishing Limited
for Bookmart Limited
Registered Number 2372865
Trading as Bookmart Limited
Desford Road
Enderby
Leicester
LE19 4AD

This edition published 2002

ISBN 1-84193-080-6

Printed and bound in China

Authors: Arthur Farndell
Martin Manser
Alice Grandison
Peter Weigall
Illustrator: Jim Hansen
Editor: Anne Fennell
Assistant Editor: Anya Martin
Designers: Tania Field & Alex Ingr
Cover designer: Susi Martin

Succeed in English

A simple and clear guide to understanding the principles of English grammar, punctuation and spelling.

Key Stage 2 upper

Ages 9 to 11 years

Arthur Farndell

Alice Grandison

Martin Manser

Peter Weigall

Capella

Introduction

English grammar, punctuation and spelling can be quite daunting to most children. Children take a while to grasp complicated rules only to find that there are so many exceptions.

By the end of Key Stage 2 children should have a good knowledge of all the eight parts of speech which comprise: verbs, nouns, adjectives, adverbs, pronouns, conjunctions, prepositions and the article. Punctuation should be at a high level and children should have at their fingertips a knowledge of where to place capital letters, commas, semi-colons, colons, apostrophes and full stops. Children should also be familiar with direct and reported speech and setting out letters, and their spelling should be accurate.

This book attempts to make the understanding of these rules of English as simple and clear as possible. The book is divided into three main sections: grammar, punctuation and spelling. It covers all topics in the Key Stage 2 from basic to high level, explaining each topic clearly. The book is laid out so that a parent can help his/her child read through and understand the principles and rules of one topic on one page, while on the opposite page are exercises to test the child's understanding of these. Marks are awarded and the child can award him/herself a star if the whole page is correct.

Your child can work through this book at his/her own speed. A topic a day can be taken, or more if the child has the energy.

Within a short period of time you should find that your child's understanding will improve and his/her marks will get better. This book can be kept as a useful guide at whatever age in life. Topics are clearly marked up and explanations are thorough yet clear.

Good luck and good practising!

Contents

the sentence

When we talk or write we do so in sentences.
A sentence is a group of words that makes complete sense on its own.
For example: • Jane finished her homework. *(complete)*
• Jane homework *(incomplete)*

All sentences begin with a **capital letter** and end with a **full stop**. (It may be a question mark or exclamation, but the full stop is still there. ? !)
For example: • **A**ndrew is a good singer**.**
• **S**wimming is good exercise**.**

> **question**

> **exclamation**

If a sentence is a question, it ends with a **question mark**.**(?)**
If it is an expression of a **strong feeling** such as surprise, pleasure, or annoyance, it ends with an **exclamation mark**. **(!)**
For example: • Do you like apples**?**
• That was such fun**!**

Types of sentence: simple, compound, & complex

> **simple sentence**

❧ A simple sentence consists of a single clause.
A clause is a part of a sentence that contains a verb.
For example: • David **entered** the room.
• **Did you remember** your gym kit?

> **compound sentence**

❧ A compound sentence consists of two main clauses joined together by a word like *and*, *but*, or *or*.
A main clause is one that makes sense on its own.
For example: • David entered the room **and** he switched on the light.
• Did you remember your gym kit **or** did you forget it?

> **complex sentence**

❧ A complex sentence consists of a **main clause** and a **subordinate clause. A subordinate clause does not make sense on its own but gives additional information about the main clause.** It begins with a conjunction like **when, because, if,** or **although**.
For example: • David turned on the light **when** he entered the room.
• Did you forget your gym kit **because** you left home in a hurry?

For each of these groups of words, write *complete* if it is a **complete sentence** or *incomplete* if it is not.

1. a big black bear _ _ _ _ _ _ _ _
2. Darren lost his pen. _ _ _ _ _ _ _ _
3. We are hungry. _ _ _ _ _ _ _ _
4. half-past eight _ _ _ _ _ _ _ _
5. My mum drives to work. _ _ _ _ _ _ _ _

For each of these sentences, decide which type it is and write a **full stop**, **question mark**, or **exclamation mark** at the end.

6. How old are you _
7. It's time for lunch _
8. What a lovely thing to say _
9. The baby fell asleep _
10. Do you have a computer at home _
11. How stupid this idea is _

Types of sentence: simple, compound and complex

Add a word - **and**, **but**, or **or** - to make each pair of simple sentences into a compound sentence.

12. Sophie ate a pizza. She drank a milk shake. _ _ _
13. Would you like to stay a while? Would you like to go home? _ _ _
14. I like carrots. I don't like broccoli. _ _ _

Add one of the **conjunctions** *when*, *because*, *if* or *although* to make each pair of clauses into a complex sentence.

15. The girl was unhappy _ _ _ _ _ _ _ _ she was being bullied at school.
16. You will be late _ _ _ _ _ _ _ _ you don't hurry.
17. _ _ _ _ _ _ _ _ I grow up, I want to be a doctor.
18. The boy left his bike outside _ _ _ _ _ _ _ _ his parents had told him not to.

Write down your score out of 18:

_____
18

When you have got this page fully correct colour in the star.

nouns

A noun is a part of speech that names a thing or a person.
Every object, place, person and idea has a name. It is through a name that everything is stored in the mind ready to be used whenever that name is spoken.

For example: If I say the word **moon**, into your mind comes all the knowledge of what the moon is and the experiences you have had of it from your life, or books or films or other images.

We have to use names for things if we are to show the difference between one thing and another. Imagine how awful it would be if you were unable to let the dinner lady know that you wanted chips and not brussel sprouts.

A noun is a naming word

A noun is used for an **object**, a **person**, an **animal**, a **place**, an **event**, or a **feeling**.

For example:
- on the **table**
- a lively **party**
- a fierce **tiger**
- small **villages**
- our new **neighbours**
- deep **despair**

Common nouns

❥ **All the things that we see, touch, smell, hear or feel** such as a table, chair, football, **are common nouns.**
For example:
- This **song** is by my favourite **singer**.
- I bought this **perfume** in a foreign **country**.
- We live in a **city**.
- I stayed in because of the **rain**.

Proper nouns

❥ **A proper noun is a noun that refers to a specific thing, place or person by name**. It *always* begins with a capital letter.
For example:
- This song is by **Madonna**.
- I spent my holidays in **Spain**.
- **Nisha** sent me a postcard from **London**.
- I stayed in on **Saturday**.

Write down the **nouns** in these sentences:

1. I left my book on the desk. _ _ _ _ _ _ _ _   _ _ _ _ _ _ _
2. My mother is a clever artist. _ _ _ _ _ _ _ _   _ _ _ _ _ _ _
3. Elephants have big ears. _ _ _ _ _ _ _ _   _ _ _ _ _ _ _
4. We took the bus to the theatre. _ _ _ _ _ _ _ _   _ _ _ _ _ _ _ _
5. The concert caused great excitement. _ _ _ _ _ _ _ _   _ _ _ _ _ _ _ _
6. The nurse bandaged his finger. _ _ _ _ _ _ _ _   _ _ _ _ _ _ _ _

Common nouns

Choose a suitable **common noun** from the list below to fill the gap in each sentence:

shock	garden	party	teacher	ducks

7. The _ _ _ _ _ _ _ _ read a story to the class.
8. Please come to my _ _ _ _ _ _ _ to celebrate my birthday.
9. The children are playing outside in the _ _ _ _ _ _ _ _ .
10. We went to the pond to feed the _ _ _ _ _ _ _ _ .
11. The sound of gunfire gave them such a _ _ _ _ _ _ _ _ .

Proper nouns

In each sentence, think of a suitable **proper noun** that could replace the **bold** words.

Paris	Spanish	January	Egypt	Robert

12. We used to live in a **hot country**. _ _ _ _ _ _ _ _
13. **My best friend** invited me to a sleepover. _ _ _ _ _ _ _ _
14. His birthday is in **the coldest month of the year**. _ _ _ _ _ _ _ _
15. **The capital of France** is a very beautiful city. _ _ _ _ _ _ _ _
16. I am learning to speak **a foreign language**. _ _ _ _ _ _ _ _

17. From the **bold** words in this description below can you identify **4 common nouns** and **4 proper nouns**?

Today **Sarah** is a very happy **girl**. It is **Monday** and her **birthday** and she is visiting **Paris**. It is a beautiful **city**. Her favourite place is the **Eiffel Tower**. It is a huge structure made of **iron** and can be seen from many miles away.

Common nouns _ _ _ _ _ _ _ _   _ _ _ _ _ _ _   _ _ _ _ _ _ _ _   _ _ _ _ _ _ _ _

Proper Nouns _ _ _ _ _ _ _ _   _ _ _ _ _ _ _   _ _ _ _ _ _ _ _   _ _ _ _ _ _ _ _

Collective nouns

❧ **A collective noun is a noun that refers to a group of people, animals or things.**

refers to a group of people, animals or things

For example:
- a **flock** of sheep
- a **pride** of lions
- a **crowd** of people
- a **gaggle** of geese
- a **swarm** of bees
- a **herd** of elephants

Collective nouns are usually treated like singular nouns. **They are usually used with singular verb forms.**

For example:
- A swarm of bees **was** buzzing around the hive.
- Our group **has** been rehearsing for the show.

Abstract nouns

refers to an idea, a feeling, a state, or a quality

❧ **An abstract noun is a noun that refers to an idea, state or a quality rather than an object.**

For example:
- I have a clever **idea**.
- They did a lot of work for world **peace**.
- We expect to be treated with **fairness**.
- All the lion wanted was **courage**.

Compound nouns

❧ **A compound noun is a noun that is made up of two other words.**

We often put two words together to make one:

For example:
- **book** and **case**: **bookcase**
- **post** and **card**: **postcard**
- Eric was a **bloodthirsty** warrior whose scarred **swordhand** clasped the blade of his sword **Foebeater**!

Collective nouns

From the list below choose a **suitable collective noun** to fit the gap in each sentence.

| plague | herd | pride | crowd |

1.   A _ _ _ _ _ _ _ of lions slept quietly under the tree.
2.   A _ _ _ _ _ _ _ of cattle was grazing in the field.
3.   A huge _ _ _ _ _ _ _ gathered to watch the fireworks display.
4.   A _ _ _ _ _ _ _ of locusts destroyed all the crops.

Write down a **suitable collective noun** in the gap.

| string | cluster | gang | shoal |

5.   a _ _ _ _ _ _ _ of fish   7.   a _ _ _ _ _ _ _ of pearls
6.   a _ _ _ _ _ _ _ of thieves   8.   a _ _ _ _ _ _ _ of diamonds

Abstract nouns

In each group of **nouns**, decide which one is an **abstract noun**.

9.   nose coat love bus   _ _ _ _ _ _ _
10. jealousy guitar bed coin   _ _ _ _ _ _ _
11. carpet ball shop stillness   _ _ _ _ _ _ _

Compound nouns

Choose the correct word from the group of words in brackets to fill the gap in order to make a **compound noun**.

12.   _ _ _ _ _ _ _ ball *(foot, toe, elbow, knee)*
13.   _ _ _ _ _ _ _ bow *(sun, rain, wind, snow)*
14.   hair _ _ _ _ _ _ _ *(comb, scissors, razor, brush)*

From the following **bold** words pick the answers to questions 16-20:
John sat by the calm **river** watching the **shoal** of **fish** swim around the **rocks**.
Peace and **quietness** filled him with **happiness** as he sat on the **towpath**.

15.   One proper noun _ _ _ _ _ _ _ _
16.   One collective noun _ _ _ _ _ _ _ _
17.   Three abstract nouns _
18.   Three common nouns _
19.   One compound noun _ _ _ _ _ _ _ _

Write down your score out of 19:

____
19

When you have got this page fully correct colour in the star.

11

nouns: singular & plural

Singular and plural nouns

❧ **A singular noun is a noun that refers to a single thing or person.**
For example: • a **car** • an **act** • one **day**

❧ **A plural noun is a noun that refers to more than one thing or person**.
For example: • two **cars** • in a few **days** • several **actors**

Making plural nouns

In most cases, you can **make a plural noun by adding s or es onto the end of a singular noun.**
For example: • a bird ... two bird**s**

   • an old church ... old church**es**

However there are some exceptions to this rule:

> **-y changes to -ies**

Where the word ends with a *y* change the *y* to *i* and add **es**
For example: • a country ... two countr**ies**

   • the sky ... two sk**ies**

   • a lady... two lad**ies**

> **-f changes to -ves**

Where the word ends with an *f* change the *f* to *v* and add **es**
For example: • a calf ... two cal**ves**

   • a leaf ... two lea**ves**

   • a shelf ... two shel**ves**

There are exceptions to this rule;

   • a roof ... two roo**fs** • a belief ... many belie**fs**

> **new form of word**

Some nouns have a completely **different plural form.**
For example: • a mouse ... two **mice**

   • one child ... all the **children**

   • a goose ... a gaggle of **geese**

> **no change**

There are some nouns which **do not change in the plural.**
For example: • a deer ... many **deer**

   • a sheep ... two **sheep**

   • a fish ... many **fish**

Singular and plural nouns

Write down the **plural noun** in each of these sentences.

1. Liam washed his face and hands. _ _ _ _ _ _ _
2. We had pie and chips for dinner. _ _ _ _ _ _ _
3. I had a scarf but no gloves. _ _ _ _ _ _ _
4. Danielle has one brother and two sisters. _ _ _ _ _ _ _
5. The pens are on the table. _ _ _ _ _ _ _
6. The Greeks sailed to Troy to rescue the lovely Helen. _ _ _ _ _ _ _

Making plural nouns

In these sentences, fill in the gap with the **plural form** of the noun.

7. The _ _ _ _ _ _ _ are playing tennis. (*girl*)
8. Tickets for _ _ _ _ _ _ _ are half price. (*child*)
9. Scotland has many beautiful _ _ _ _ _ _ _. (*beach*)
10. My _ _ _ _ _ _ _ are cold. (*foot*)
11. Two _ _ _ _ _ _ _ broke into the shop. (*man*)
12. The teacher had many _ _ _ _ _ _ _. (pupil)
13. The _ _ _ _ _ _ _ in the choir sang beautifully. (lady)

In these sentences, **fill in the plural form of the noun** that appears in brackets after the sentence.

14. The place was swarming with _ _ _ _ _ _ _ . (fly)
15. Foxes and _ _ _ _ _ _ _ belong to the dog family. (wolf)
16. The farmer keeps cows and _ _ _ _ _ _ _ . (sheep)
17. Cats chase birds and _ _ _ _ _ _ _ . (mouse)
18. The _ _ _ _ _ _ _ and forks are kept in this drawer. (knife)
19. My brother keeps tropical _ _ _ _ _ _ _ . (fish)
20. Two_ _ _ _ _ _ _ are equal to four quarters. (half)
21. We saw a herd of _ _ _ _ _ _ _ on the hillside. (deer)
22. _ _ _ _ _ _ _ have very soft skin. (baby)
23. Brush your _ _ _ _ _ _ _ before you go to bed. (tooth)
24. _ _ _ _ _ _ _ 's football is becoming popular. (woman)

Write down your score out of 24:

_____
24

When you have got this page fully correct colour in the star.

13

verbs

A verb is a *part of speech* that tells you what a person or thing does or how they are.

A verb expresses the action

Every complete sentence and every clause includes a verb. If it has no verb it is not a proper sentence.

We see and take part in thousands of actions every day.

ways we speak

We **talk**, **scream**, **whisper**, **shout**, **question**, **tell**, and communicate in many other ways!

ways we move

We **walk**, **run**, **jump**, **skip**, **shuffle**, **leap**, **swim**, **jog**, **cycle**, **drive**, and do a thousand other actions as well!

ways we feel

We **laugh**, **cry**, **enjoy**, **annoy**, **love**, **think**, **hate**, and so on!

Present, past, and future tenses

The tense of a verb tells you when its action takes place – in the present, the past, or the future.

present tense

❥ **The present tense tells you about what is happening now.**
For example: • Asia **is** beautiful.
• Paul **is** doing his homework.

past tense

❥ **The past tense tells you about what happened in the past.**
For example: • My grandmother **was** beautiful.
• Paul **did** his homework.

future tense

❥ **The future tense tells you about what will happen in the future.**
For example: • You **will be** beautiful when you grow up.
• I **will do** my homework after my dance class.

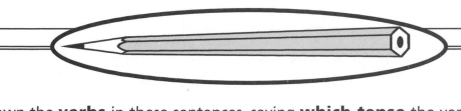
Write down the **verbs** in these sentences, saying **which tense** the verb is written in.

1. Kerry goes to karate classes. _ _ _ _ _ _ _ _ _ _ _ _ _ _
2. Chloe will write to a girl in France. _ _ _ _ _ _ _ _ _ _ _ _ _ _
3. The baby was tired. _ _ _ _ _ _ _ _ _ _ _ _ _ _
4. Rajesh will fly to India on holiday. _ _ _ _ _ _ _ _ _ _ _ _ _ _
5. The shops are very busy. _ _ _ _ _ _ _ _ _ _ _ _ _ _
6. We stayed in a hotel. _ _ _ _ _ _ _ _ _ _ _ _ _ _

Present, past, and future tenses

In each sentence, change the verb **from the present** tense **to the past** tense.

7. She jogs every day. _ _ _ _ _ _ _
8. I bake scones. _ _ _ _ _ _ _
9. His shoes are dirty. _ _ _ _ _ _ _
10. Megan looks sad. _ _ _ _ _ _ _
11. Ben sings with a band. _ _ _ _ _ _ _
12. My friend lives in Liverpool. _ _ _ _ _ _ _

In each sentence, change the verb **from present** tense into the **future**.

13. I am cooking the dinner. _ _ _ _ _ _ _ _
14. Peter plays with his boat. _ _ _ _ _ _ _ _
15. Anne sings in a concert. _ _ _ _ _ _ _ _
16. Mary dances with her sister _ _ _ _ _ _ _ _

In each sentence, fill in the **correct tense** of the verb that appears in brackets after the sentence.

17. I _ _ _ _ _ _ _ _ my room tomorrow. (*tidy*)
18. Last week we _ _ _ _ _ _ _ _ to the cinema. (*go*)
19. I felt sad yesterday but I _ _ _ _ _ _ _ _ happy today. (*feel*)
20. I _ _ _ _ _ _ _ _ eleven on my next birthday. (*be*)
21. Jasmina _ _ _ _ _ _ _ _ to school while Anna took the bus. (*walk*)
22. Adam _ _ _ _ _ _ _ _ football while James was doing his homework. (*play*)
23. Jamie _ _ _ _ _ _ _ _ the office and went home to his wife. *(leave)*
24. December _ _ _ _ _ _ _ _ a winter month. *(be)*

Write down your score out of 24:

_____
24

When you have got this page fully correct colour in the star.

15

different voices

Active voice and passive voice

There are two ways of expressing the action of a verb – the *active voice* and the *passive voice*.

Active voice

❧ The active voice of a verb tells you that **someone or something does something**. The **subject** of the verb **carries out the action** of the verb.

For example: • The dog **bit** the boy.
• The cat **sat** on the mat.
• The mechanic **is fixing** the car.
• The girls **are arranging** the flowers.
• Rachel **has won** the contest.
• Paul **will complete** the work.

Passive voice

❧ The passive voice of a verb tells you that **something is done by someone or something**. The **subject** of the verb **has the action done to them.**

For example: • The boy **was bitten**.
• The mat **was sat** on.
• The car **is being fixed**.
• The flowers **are being arranged**.
• The contest **has been won**.
• The work **will be completed**.

using 'by'

Sometimes the person or thing that carries out the action of the verb is shown after the verb, using the word ***by.***
For example: • The boy was bitten **by the dog**.
• The mat was sat on **by the cat**.
• The car is being fixed **by the mechanic.**
• The flowers are being arranged **by the girls**.
• The contest has been won **by Rachel**.
• The work will be completed **by Paul**.

Active voice and passive voice

Write out the verb in the sentence and say whether the **verb** is *active* or *passive*.

1. The girl broke the vase. _
2. The vase was broken by the girl. _
3. This picture is being painted by my dad. _ _ _ _ _ _ _ _ _ _ _ _ _ _ _ _ _
4. My dad paints a picture of a dog. _
5. He sang a song. _
6. The song was sung by a beautiful woman. _ _ _ _ _ _ _ _ _ _ _ _ _ _ _ _ _
7. The money was stolen by the thieves. _ _ _ _ _ _ _ _ _ _ _ _ _ _ _ _ _
8. Jane will swim in the race tomorrow. _ _ _ _ _ _ _ _ _ _ _ _ _ _ _ _ _ _

Passive voice

Change each sentence around so that the **verb** is in the **passive** voice. Remember that you will have to change the order of the words and use *by* to show the person or thing that carries out the **action** or the **verb**.

9. The cat chased the mouse.
   _ _ _ _ _ _ _ _ **The mouse was chased by the cat** _ _ _ _ _ _ _ _
10. Roald Dahl wrote this book.
    _
11. My Gran knitted my sweater.
    _
12. Robbie Williams recorded this song.
    _
13. The red team beat the green team.
    _
14. David Coulthard drove the winning car.
    _
15. Jasmine and Sam helped the teacher.
    _
16. The builders will complete the house tomorrow.
    _

Write down your score out of 16:

_____

16

When you have got this page fully correct colour in the star.

17

auxiliary verbs

the word 'auxiliary'

Auxiliary **is not a word we use often but it means** *helping.* It helps a verb go into different tenses or times and we use these words very often although we may not realise it.

Forming tense and voice

be, have, do, will

Here are some auxiliary verbs which are **used to form tenses and the passive voice.**

For example: • I **am waiting** for a bus.
• The letter **was written** in green ink. *(passive voice)*
• Everyone **has gone** home.
• All the cakes **have been sold**. *(passive voice)*
• **Do** you **like** pasta?
• I **did** not **take** your calculator.
• I **think** it **will rain** tomorrow.

In the first three examples the words *waiting*, *written* and *gone* are forms of the main verbs. The words *am*, *was*, *has*, are all **helping** or **auxiliary** verbs.

Adding to the meaning

➤ **Other auxiliary verbs add to the meaning of the verb phrase.**

can, could, may, might, must, ought to, should

For example: • I **can reach** the top shelf.
• **Could** you **help** me with this problem, please?
• **May** I **leave** the table?
• I **might go** to the game if I can get a ticket.
• You **must do** your maths homework by Thursday.
• You really **ought to wear** a cycling helmet.
• You **should cross** at the pelican crossing.

Forming tense and voice

From the **auxiliary verbs** below, choose a suitable one to fill the gap in each sentence.

| am | has | do | will | was |

1. Craig _ _ _ _ _ _ _ _ done the washing-up.

2. I _ _ _ _ _ _ _ _ going to the library.

3. _ _ _ _ _ _ _ _ they now live near here?

4. Tomorrow we _ _ _ _ _ _ _ _ go shopping.

5. The jumble sale _ _ _ _ _ _ _ _ organised by the Parents' Association.

6. Katie _ _ _ _ _ _ _ _ been punished for telling lies.

7. I _ _ _ _ _ _ _ _ not like going to the dentist.

Adding to the meaning

From the **auxiliary verbs** below, choose a suitable one to fill the gap in each sentence.

| can | could | may | might | ought | should | must |

8. The baby _ _ _ _ _ _ _ _ say a few words now.

9. You _ _ _ _ _ _ _ _ go home if you have finished your work.

10. _ _ _ _ _ _ _ _ I please borrow your rubber?

11. You _ _ _ _ _ _ _ _ pay your deposit by 30 September if you want
     to go on the school trip to Paris.

12. We _ _ _ _ _ _ _ _ go to Florida or maybe we will go to France.

13. You _ _ _ _ _ _ _ _ to wear a warm jumper as it is cold.

14. We _ _ _ _ _ _ _ _ arrive in five minutes.

Write down a. the form of the **main verb** and b. the **auxiliary verb**.

15. I will go to the cinema. a. _ _ _ _ _ _ _ _ b._ _ _ _ _ _ _

16. They had listened to the lecturer. a._ _ _ _ _ _ _ _ b._ _ _ _ _ _ _ _

17. You ought to dress warmly. a. _ _ _ _ _ _ _ _ b. _ _ _ _ _ _ _ _

18. She will be happy about that. a. _ _ _ _ _ _ _ _ b. _ _ _ _ _ _ _ _

19. The children must learn their grammar. a. _ _ _ _ _ _ _ _ b. _ _ _ _ _ _ _ _

Write down
your score
out of 19:

_____
19

When you
have got this
page fully
correct colour
in the star.

19

subject, verb, object

When we look at a sentence we first find the verb:
Giggs scored. The verb is *scored*.
We then ask ourselves: who scored? The answer is *Giggs*.
Giggs is the subject of the sentence.

subject

❯ The subject, in an active sentence, is a person or thing that carries out the action of a verb. The subject can be a noun, a pronoun, or a noun phrase. A noun phrase is a group of words that includes a noun and that is treated as a noun.
For example: • **Chocolate** is delicious.
• **Louis** plays chess.
• **We** went bowling.
• **All the children** have gone home. (*noun phrase*)

In most sentences the subject comes before the verb, but in questions the verb comes before the subject.
For example: • **I** am ready.   • Are **you** ready?

Object and verb

object

❯ The object is a person or thing that the action of a verb is done to. It is what is directly affected by the action. The object can be a noun, a pronoun, or a noun phrase. The object usually comes after the verb in a sentence.
For example: • Shereen does not eat **meat**.
• I met **them** at the concert on Friday.
• We saw **lions** and **tigers** at the zoo.
• Have you done your **French homework**?

Subject and Verb agreement

verb agreement

❯ The verb should agree with the subject of the sentence.

A **singular noun** is used with a **singular verb** form.
For example: • A banana **is** yellow.   • This man **drives** too fast.

A **plural noun** is used with a **plural verb** form.
For example: • Bananas **are** yellow.
• These **men drive** too fast.

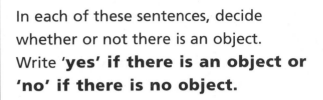

In each of these sentences, decide whether or not there is an object. Write **'yes' if there is an object or 'no' if there is no object.**

1. We enjoyed the game. _ _ _
2. The boy rode his bike. _ _ _
3. I fell. _ _ _
4. The guests arrived. _ _ _

Subject and verb

Circle the **verb** and the **subject** in each sentence.

5. Lauren takes piano lessons.
6. The test was taken yesterday.
7. Does the girl drink milk?
8. Computer games are cheap in this shop.
9. We love football.
10. The rose is beautiful.

Object and verb

Draw a circle round the **object** in each sentence.

11. Steve married Melanie.
12. A big boy pushed me.
13. We had a snowball fight.
14. Did you draw this picture?
15. Martin drove his car.
16. She brushed her teeth?

Verb agreement

In these sentences, fill in the **correct form of the verb** that appears in brackets after the sentence.

17. Apples _ _ _ _ _ _ _ on trees. (grow)
18. My brother _ _ _ _ _ _ _ rugby. (play)
19. My sisters _ _ _ _ _ _ _ _ volleyball. (play)
20. The film _ _ _ _ _ _ _ at two o'clock. (start)

Agreement

In this paragraph there are six mistakes where the **verb** does not agree with the **noun**. Write the **correct form** of each in the space provided below.

Rebecca and Harriet **is** best friends. The girls live in the same street and they **goes** to the same school. Harriet's mother **are** taking the girls to a concert. The car **have** broken down and the girls **is** worried in case they miss their favourite band. Luckily a bus **come** along and they arrive at the concert just in time.

21. _____
22. _____
23. _____
24. _____
25. _____
26. _____

Write down your score out of 26:

___
26

When you have got this page fully correct colour in the star.

pronouns

A pronoun is used instead of a noun

It is often used in order to avoid repeating a noun that has already been mentioned.

For example:
- Tim found a purse. **He** took **it** to the police station.
- The woman picked up the letter and opened **it**.

Personal pronouns

❧ Personal pronouns **refer to people**, apart from **it**, which refers to a **thing**, and **they**, which can refer to **people or things.**

For example:
- **She** is my friend.
- Take these books and put **them** on the shelf.
- Megan borrowed my video and watched **it**.

I, you, he, she, it, we, they are used as the **subject of a sentence**;

me, you, him, her, it, us, them are used as the **object of a verb or preposition**.

Possessive pronouns

❧ Possessive pronouns **show who something belongs to** or is connected with. The possessive pronouns are *mine*, *yours*, *his*, *hers*, *its*, *ours*, and *theirs*.

For example:
- If you don't have a barbecue, you can borrow **ours**.
- I see your name on the list but I don't see **mine**.

Relative pronouns

❧ The relative pronouns *who, whom, whose, which,* and *that* introduce a relative clause. **A relative clause is a kind of subordinate clause that gives you more information about the noun or noun phrase that comes before it.**
Who, *whom*, and *whose* refer to people; *which* refers to things; *that* can refer to people or things.

For example:
- This is the girl **who** painted this beautiful picture.
- I met my American cousin, **whom** I had never seen before.
- We had lasagne, **which** is my favourite food.
- That was the nurse **that** bandaged my finger.

Write down the **pronouns** in these sentences.

1. Bananas are delicious and they don't cost much. _ _ _ _ _ _ _ _
2. When my sister grows up, she wants to be a singer. _ _ _ _ _ _ _ _
3. The princess kissed the frog and it turned into a prince. _ _ _ _ _ _ _ _

Personal pronouns

In each of these sentences, replace the blank with a suitable **personal pronoun**.

4. Can _ _ _ _ _ _ _ borrow this CD, please?
5. Finish your worksheet and hand _ _ _ _ _ _ _ _ in.
6. I asked my parents if I could help _ _ _ _ _ _ _ _ with the gardening.

Possessive pronouns

In each of these sentences, replace the blank with a suitable **possessive pronoun**.

7. Give me your phone number and I will give you _ _ _ _ _ _ _ _.
8. I couldn't find my calculator but Ahmed let me use _ _ _ _ _ _ _ _.
9. Sean ate all the sweets because his sisters didn't want _ _ _ _ _ _ _ _.

Relative pronouns

In each of these sentences, replace the blank with a suitable **relative pronoun**.

10. The boy _ _ _ _ _ _ _ _ broke the window ran away.
11. We are going to Rome, _ _ _ _ _ _ _ _ is the capital of Italy.
12. In the summer he met the woman _ _ _ _ _ _ _ _ he later married.

Pronouns

Pick out **three personal pronouns**, **three possessive pronouns**, and **three relative pronouns** in this paragraph and write them in the spaces provided below.

In the summer I am going to visit friends of mine who live just outside New York. They live in a big house with a swimming pool. The house is much bigger than ours. A neighbour of theirs will take us to see the Empire State Building, which is the tallest building in New York.

13. Personal pronouns _ _ _ _ _ _ _ _ _ _ _ _ _ _ _ _ _ _ _ _ _ _
14. Possessive pronouns _ _ _ _ _ _ _ _ _ _ _ _ _ _ _ _ _ _ _ _
15. Relative pronouns _ _ _ _ _ _ _ _ _ _ _ _ _ _ _ _ _ _ _ _ _ _ _

Write down your score out of 15:

_____
15

When you have got this page fully correct colour in the star.

23

adjectives

An adjective is a part of speech that describes a noun. It tells you more about a person, thing, place, or event.

> ## An adjective describes a noun or a pronoun

Adjectives can tell you what a person or thing looks like, sounds like, or feels like.

For example: • Anil is a **handsome** boy.
• We heard a **loud** bang.
• They were **happy**.

They can tell you **what kind of thing something is, what kind of person someone is,** and so on.
For example: • Louise is a **clever** girl.
• Glasgow is a **busy** city.

Comparatives and Superlatives

> comparative

❧ **is the form of an adjective that you use to say that a person or thing has *more of a certain quality* than another.** You do this by adding *er* onto the end of the adjective if it is a short word, or by using *more* before the adjective if it is a long word.
For example: • Ryan is **taller** than Emma.
• Najma is **more beautiful** than her sister.

> superlative

❧ **is the form of an adjective that you use to say that a person or thing has *more of a certain quality* than all others in a group or category.** You do this by adding *est* to a short adjective, or by using *most* before a long adjective.
For example: • This is the **quickest** way to the cinema.
• This is the **most exciting** book I have ever read.

Adjective phrases

❧ **An adjective phrase is a group of words that includes an adjective and that describes a noun or pronoun.**
For example: • The answer was **very obvious**.
• I was **totally exhausted** after the race.
• Her story was **hard to believe**.

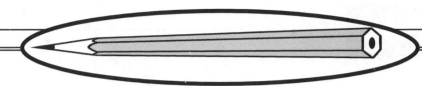

Write down the **adjectives** in these sentences.

1. We had a hot meal and a cool drink.   1 _ _ _ _ _ _ _ _
   2 _ _ _ _ _ _ _ _

2. I wrote a long letter to my elderly aunt.   1 _ _ _ _ _ _ _ _
   2 _ _ _ _ _ _ _ _

3. The girl felt nervous before the important exam.   1 _ _ _ _ _ _ _ _
   2 _ _ _ _ _ _ _ _

4. I was tired and my back was sore.   1 _ _ _ _ _ _ _ _
   2 _ _ _ _ _ _ _ _

5. Your new dress is gorgeous.   1 _ _ _ _ _ _ _ _
   2 _ _ _ _ _ _ _ _

6. The angry teacher punished the naughty boy.   1 _ _ _ _ _ _ _ _
   2 _ _ _ _ _ _ _ _

Comparisons

In these comparisons, fill in the correct form of the **adjective**
that appears in brackets after the sentence.

7. A mouse is _ _ _ _ _ _ _ _ than a cat. *(small)*

8. His second attempt was _ _ _ _ _ _ _ _ than his first. *(successful)*

9. Jamal is the _ _ _ _ _ _ _ _ player in the team. *(skilful)*

10. Mount Everest is the _ _ _ _ _ _ _ _ mountain in the world. *(high)*

11. He bought the _ _ _ _ _ _ _ _ camera in the shop. *(expensive)*

12. Paul is _ _ _ _ _ _ _ _ than Mark but Luke is the _ _ _ _ _ _ _ _ of
    the three boys. *(young)*

Adjective phrases

Write down the **adjective phrases** in these sentences.

13. I hope you have a very happy birthday. _ _ _ _ _ _ _ _

14. The children were rather hungry. _ _ _ _ _ _ _ _

15. The instructions are easy to understand. _ _ _ _ _ _ _ _

16. These shoes are surprisingly comfortable. _ _ _ _ _ _ _ _

Write down
your score
out of 16:

_____
16

When you
have got this
page fully
correct colour
in the star.

adverbs

An adverb is a part of speech that tells you more about a verb.

An adverb describes a verb

❯ **An adverb tells you where, why, or how much something happens or is done.**

Many adverbs are formed by adding *ly* onto the end of an adjective.

For example:
- The boy **kindly** carried the old lady's bags.
- It was **strangely** quiet in the village.
- We ate our sandwiches **extremely** quickly.

adverbs of manner

tell you *how* something happens or is done.

For example:
- The children were **smartly** dressed.
- If you walk **fast**, you will catch the bus.
- He is **quietly** confident.

Other examples: **sadly, roughly, safely, happily, slowly, neatly**

adverbs of time

tell you *when* something happens or is done.

For example:
- Our guests arrived **yesterday**.
- The holidays will **soon** be over.

Other examples: **late, today, early, always, after, now, never**

adverbs of place

tell you *where* something happens or is done.

For example:
- Come **here**.
- My aunt and uncle live **nearby**.

Other examples: **there, near, far, everywhere, out**

adverbs of degree

tell you *how much* something happens or is done.

For example:
- The girl was **slightly** injured in the accident.
- We were all **very** tired.

Other examples: **too, slightly, extremely, very, mostly**

Pick out the **verbs** and **adverbs** in these sentences.

1. Carefully cut out the figures.   v_ _ _ _ _ _   adv_ _ _ _ _ _
2. The man was badly hurt in the accident.   v_ _ _ _ _ _   adv_ _ _ _ _ _
3. You must answer the question honestly.   v_ _ _ _ _ _   adv_ _ _ _ _ _
4. This band plays superbly.   v_ _ _ _ _ _   adv_ _ _ _ _ _

Adverbs of manner

Choose a suitable **adverb of manner** to fill the gap in each sentence.

quickly	brightly	angrily	warmly

5. The stars were shining _ _ _ _ _ _ _ in a clear sky.
6. The teacher shouted _ _ _ _ _ _ _ at the naughty children.
7. Wrap up _ _ _ _ _ _ _ before you go out in the cold.
8. He ran _ _ _ _ _ _ _ to catch the train.

Adverbs of time

Choose a suitable **adverb of time** to fill the gap in each sentence.

never	tomorrow	now

9. We will go into town _ _ _ _ _ _ _ after school.
10. I used to dislike football but I like it _ _ _ _ _ _ _.
11. I have been to France but I have _ _ _ _ _ _ _ been to Italy.

Adverbs of place

Choose a suitable **adverb of place** to fill the gap in each sentence.

outside	far	there

12. I'm going _ _ _ _ _ _ _ for some fresh air.
13. I am going to Birmingham because my Gran lives _ _ _ _ _ _ _.
14. Don't go too _ _ _ _ _ _ _ away from the house.

Adverbs of degree

Choose a suitable **adverb of degree** to fill the gap in each sentence.

extremely	too

15. It was _ _ _ _ _ _ _ cold to go out without a coat.
16. Sharks have _ _ _ _ _ _ _ sharp teeth.

Write down your score out of 16:

____
16

When you have got this page fully correct colour in the star.

prepositions and conjunctions

Prepositions

A preposition shows the relationship between one word and another.

➤ A preposition is a part of speech that shows how the **noun or pronoun that comes after it is related to the verb, noun, or pronoun that comes before it.**

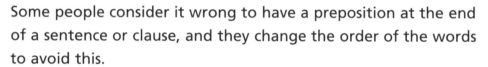

For example: • The book is **on** the table.
           • I saw a film **about** dinosaurs.
           • I have a gift **for** you.
           • Will you share it **with** me?

Some people consider it wrong to have a preposition at the end of a sentence or clause, and they change the order of the words to avoid this.

For example: This is the man **to whom** I spoke.
           For whom are you waiting?

If changing the order of the words makes the sentence sound awkward, it is best to leave the preposition at the end.

For example: This is the man **that I spoke to**.
           Who are you waiting **for**?

Conjunctions

A conjunction is a part of speech that joins words, phrases and clauses.

For example: I went to the shop **and** I bought a magazine.
           You will pass the exam **if** you study hard.
           The weather was cold **but** dry.

The conjunction that you choose can change the meaning of a sentence.

For example: • I went home **when** it started to rain.
           • I went home **before** it started to rain.
           • I went home **because** it started to rain.

Prepositions

Write down the **prepositions** in these sentences.

1. I'm writing a letter to Neil. _ _ _ _ _ _ _

2. We had cereal for breakfast. _ _ _ _ _ _ _

3. She met him at the station. _ _ _ _ _ _ _

4. Sit here beside me. _ _ _ _ _ _ _

Change the order of the words in each sentence to **avoid having a preposition at the end.**

5. Here is a box that you can keep your pencils in.

    _

6. Who are you searching for?

    _

7. I met the girl that I go to school with.

    _

8. Find a peg which you can hang your coat on.

    _

Conjunctions

Write down the **conjunctions** in these sentences.

9. Sugar is sweet but lemons are sour. _ _ _ _ _ _ _ _

10. Her hair is soft and shiny. _ _ _ _ _ _ _ _

11. I woke up when the alarm went off. _ _ _ _ _ _ _ _

12. Would you like an apple or an orange? _ _ _ _ _ _ _ _

Write down a suitable **conjunction** to fill the gap in each sentence.

13. I like cats _ _ _ _ _ _ _ _ I don't like dogs.

14. Joel was late for school _ _ _ _ _ _ _ _ he overslept.

15. You must wait here _ _ _ _ _ _ _ _ your name is called.

16. She rang _ _ _ _ _ _ _ _ you were out.

Write down
your score
out of 16:

_____
16

When you
have got this
page fully
correct colour
in the star.

29

articles

The articles are the words *a*, *an*, and *the*.

A part of speech that comes before a noun

➤ **An article is a part of speech that comes before a noun, sometimes with other words in between.**

For example:
- He was wearing **a** jumper.
- She ate **an** ice lolly.
- They called out **the** doctor.
- **The** little girl was crying.
- That was **a** very funny joke.

The definite and indefinite articles

The definite article is *the*. The indefinite articles are *a* and *an*.

the definite article

➤ **The definite article refers to a particular person or thing.**

For example:
- I am going to **the** dentist.
- We caught **the** eight o'clock bus.
- That is **the** woman who lives next door.

the indefinite article

➤ **The indefinite articles refer to a person or thing in a less specific way.**

A is used before a consonant sound.

An is used before a word beginning with a vowel sound or a silent *h*.

For example:
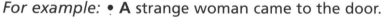
- **A** strange woman came to the door.
- The hen laid **an** egg.
- He is **an** honest man.
- I am saving up for **a** personal CD player.

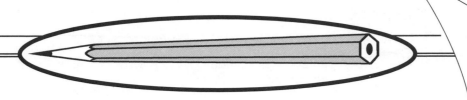

Write down the **articles** in these sentences.

1. We have a pet dog. _ _ _ _ _ _ _
2. Then the phone rang. _ _ _ _ _ _ _
3. They were in a terrible hurry. _ _ _ _ _ _ _
4. This is an emergency. _ _ _ _ _ _ _
5. Who won the Cup Final? _ _ _ _ _ _ _

The definite and indefinite articles

Suggest a suitable **article**, either **definite** or **indefinite**, to fill the gap in each sentence.

6. Isn't that _ _ _ _ _ _ _ man who works in the newsagent's?
7. What _ _ _ _ _ _ _ cute little kitten!
8. I sent you _ _ _ _ _ _ _ e-mail.
9. That's _ _ _ _ _ _ _ interesting idea.
10. The blue whale is _ _ _ _ _ _ _ largest animal in the world.

Suggest a suitable **noun**, or **noun phrase**, to fill the gap after the **article** in each sentence.

| police station | taxi | early night | hour | radiator |

11. Put your wet gloves on the _ _ _ _ _ _ _ _ .
12. I'm going to have an _ _ _ _ _ _ _ _ _ _ _ since I have to get up at six a.m.
13. The man was arrested and taken to the _ _ _ _ _ _ _ _ _ _ _ _ _ .
14. We ordered a _ _ _ _ _ _ _ _ _ _ _ _ to take us to the airport.
15. The flight was an _ _ _ _ _ _ _ _ _ _ _ late.

Write down
your score
out of 15:

___
15

When you
have got this
page fully
correct colour
in the star.

31

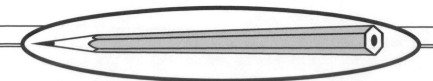

Revision

Add what is needed to change each group of words into a **complete sentence.**

sing   wagged   eat

1. the little white dog its tail
2. vegetarians no meat
3. the choir Christmas carols

State which sentence is **simple, compound** or **complex.**

4. The boys went into town and bought a football. _ _ _ _ _ _ _
5. The sun shines brightly.

   _ _ _ _ _ _ _ _ _
6. We can stay here for a while although it is late.

   _ _ _ _ _ _ _ _ _

Nouns

Draw a circle round the **noun** and underline the **abstract noun** in each group of words.

7. tiny   listen   chocolate   happiness
8. beauty   flower   whenever   bring
9. conversation   forget   fluffy   illness

In each sentence, change the incorrect singular noun into its **correct plural noun**.

10. Rebecca had two cheese <u>sandwich</u> for lunch.
11. Always brush your <u>tooth</u> before you go to bed.

12. The two <u>wife</u> met their husbands at the restaurant.

Verbs

For each sentence, write down which **tense – present, past, or future –** the **verb** is in.

13. My uncle came to our house last Saturday. _ _ _ _ _ _ _ _
14. Next year we will go to Spain on holiday. _ _ _ _ _ _ _ _
15. Pizza is my favourite food.

    _ _ _ _ _ _ _

In each sentence, fill in the gap with a suitable **verb**, and say whether it is in the **active voice** or the **passive voice**.

cut   was scored   was built

16. I _ _ _ _ my finger with a sharp knife. _____
17. The winning goal _ _ _ _ _ _ _ _ by Michael Owen. _____
18. Our house _ _ _ _ _ _ _ _ in 1960. _____

In each sentence, fill in the gap with a suitable **auxiliary verb** .

have   will   can   must

19. I _ _ _ _ _ _ see you next Monday.
20. We _ _ _ _ _ _ already seen that film.

21. You absolutely _ _ _ _ _ _ finish your topic by Friday.
22. If I _ _ _ _ _ _ come to the party, I will.

Pronouns

In each sentence, fill in the gap with a suitable **pronoun – personal**, **possessive**, or **relative**.

23. My brother, _ _ _ _ _ is younger than me, is taller than me.
24. Your socks have holes in

    _ _ _ _ _ _ .
25. I've finished my lunch and you haven't even started _ _ _ _ yet.

Adjectives

Write down the **comparative** and **superlative** of each of these **adjectives**.

26. rough _ _ _ _ _ _ _

    _ _ _ _ _ _ _
27. big _ _ _ _ _ _ _ _ _ _ _ _
28. wonderful _ _ _ _ _ _ _ _ _ _ _ _

    _ _ _ _ _ _ _ _ _ _ _ _

Adverbs

Draw a circle round the **adverb** in each group of words.

29. soon delivery pale wander
30. dictionary squeeze nobody sadly
31. country evolve everywhere funny

Prepositions

Draw a circle round the **preposition** in each group of words.

32. fifteen above abroad long
33. drive life to two
34. under show free circle

Conjunctions

Draw a circle round the **conjunction** in each group of words.

35. because become better beyond
36. but button butt butter
37. allow alter although alert

Articles

In each sentence, fill in the gap with a suitable **article**, either **definite** or **indefinite**.

38. I woke up in _ _ _ _ middle of the night.
39. I woke up in _ _ _ _ cold sweat.
40. I woke up in _ _ _ _ empty room.

Introduction + capital letters

When we talk, we talk in sentences which are complete thoughts in words. When we write down words and sentences we have to show where one sentence ends and another begins. When we have shown where the complete sentence is, we must show the different parts of the sentence so that the meaning is clear and simple.

The marks we put down on paper to show the different parts of the sentence are called marks of **punctuation**. This word *punctuation* comes from the Latin word *punctum* meaning *point* or *mark*. There are many marks of punctuation such as **full stops**, **commas**, **apostrophes** and **speech marks**.

There are other types of punctuation which are not marks but are nevertheless important such as **capital letters**, **indentations** and **paragraphs** which all show the meaning of what is being said when written down.

The **first letter** of every sentence begins with a **capital letter**. *For example:* The moon was full that night.

The first letter of every proper noun, the particular name of a person, place, title or thing, begins with a **capital letter**.

For example: Queen Elizabeth lives in many great houses – Windsor Castle, Balmoral, Sandringham and Buckingham Palace.

Check your alphabet!

Here is the alphabet which shows the difference between capital letters and small (or lower case) letters:

Lower Case Letters:

a b c d e f g h i j k l m n o p q r s t u v w x y z

CAPITAL LETTERS:

A B C D E F G H I J K L M N O P Q R S T U V W X Y Z

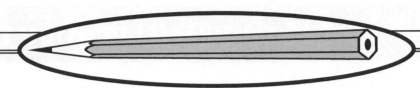

Test your alphabet writing:

1.   Write these letters in **Capital Letters:**

   a _ _ _   c _ _ _   f _ _ _   g _ _ _   l _ _ _   e _ _ _

   o _ _ _   t _ _ _   s _ _ _   j _ _ _   o _ _ _   n _ _ _

   x _ _ _   y _ _ _   z _ _ _   b _ _ _   d _ _ _   q _ _ _

2.   Write these letters in the **lower case:**

   B _ _ _   C _ _ _   J _ _ _   U _ _ _   Y _ _ _   R _ _ _

   I _ _ _   M _ _ _   Q _ _ _   H _ _ _   F _ _ _   K _ _ _

Write out these sentences putting the **first letters** of the sentence and **proper names** into **capital letters.**

3.   jack and sam went to london.

   _

4.   jane and samina went shopping in oxford street.

   _

5.   the titanic was on its way from liverpool to new york.

   _

6.   cardiff is the capital of wales; edinburgh is the capital of scotland;
        paris is the capital of france and madrid is the capital of spain.

   _

   _

Write down
your score
out of 6:

$\dfrac{}{6}$

When you
have got this
page fully
correct colour
in the star.

full stop, question and exclamation mark

full stop

A full stop looks like this: .

It is a round dot written at the end of a sentence and indicates the end of a complete thought.
For example: • The sun is shining brightly**.**
This is a complete thought in words and it ends with the full stop.

Without punctuation we would soon get very confused and out of breath. Often when you are reading a sentence aloud, the **punctuation marks will tell you where to breathe** so that the sense of the sentence is not lost.

Hearing when one sentence ends and another begins.
When you are writing, it is much easier to hear when one sentence ends and another begins if you read your words aloud. You can then hear the beginnings and the ends by the sense of the sentence.

question mark

➤ **When we want to know something we ask questions. When writing down a question, the sentence *begins with a capital letter* and *ends with* ?
– a question mark.**
For example: • What time is it **?**
                • Where did you go yesterday **?**
                • How many chocolate biscuits did you eat **?**

exclamation mark

➤ **When you want to show that someone is speaking *with strong feeling, you end the sentence with an exclamation mark.***
An exclamation mark **!** – is a full stop with a vertical line above it. There is a small space between the line and the circle.
For example: • How beautiful that picture is **!**
                • He fell backwards into the pond **!**
                • What a magnificent palace that is **!**

Often **commands** will be followed by an exclamation mark:
For example: • "Get out of here, at once **!** " shouted the captain.
                • Abandon ship **!**
                • Do not cross the red lights **!**

With a coloured pencil mark these sentences with **capital letters** and **full stops**.

1. the world is round like a ball

2. the earth goes round the sun in a year

3. the moon orbits the earth

4. compared to the sun the earth is a small speck

Read these sentences and **mark with a coloured pencil** where **full stops** and **capital letters** should be. There should be five capital letters and five full stops. *Do not forget: read the sentences aloud to hear where they begin and end!*

5. once people thought the world was flat they thought the sun was a fiery chariot driven across the sky by the god Helios he drove it out from the east in the morning he raced it across the sky during the day in the evening it sank below the horizon

Mark these **questions** with **capital letters** and **question marks**.

6. why did you put mustard in the custard

7. where did you hide when the monster came

8. how can you tell

9. will it stop raining

Mark these sentences with **capital letters** and **full stops** or **exclamation marks** if you think the sentence expresses a strong feeling.

10. what an expensive meal that was

11. the plane took off

12. it turned three somersaults and flew upside down

13. it flew high into the sky

Mark these sentences with **capital letters, full stops, question marks** or **exclamation marks**.

14. the titanic sailed across the atlantic

15. what's happened

16. we're going down

Write down your score out of 16:

——— 16

When you have got this page fully correct colour in the star.

37

commas

We have looked at the sentence and seen where it begins and ends. **Now we look at the inside of a sentence.** A sentence may be very short or it may be very long with many different parts to it.

Commas are the main division within a sentence

Commas look like very small nines which sit on and just below the bottom of a line close to the base of the letters. A *comma* – **,**

A comma has many uses. Here are some of the main ones:

➤ **A. Commas are used to separate a list of words or groups of words.**

For example: You will need pencils, paper, a ruler, rubber and compass.

Note: that the last two words are joined by **and** and *not* a comma.

David went down to the stream, chose some smooth pebbles, put four of them into his pouch **and** put the fifth into his sling.

Goliath walked down the hill, over the stream, up the pebbly bank **and** stood on a great boulder.

➤ **B. Commas are used to separate introductory words, or groups of words** especially at the beginning of a sentence.

For example: When the rain stops, we will go out into the fields.
If you do that again, I will be very cross!
Although the hour had struck, we went on working.
Crying bitterly, the young boy rubbed his eyes.

➤ **C. Commas are used to mark off the person being addressed:**

For example: "Row as hard as you can, my men!" begged Odysseus.
"Odysseus, you are truly a hero!" agreed his men.
"You, Cyclops, are cruel and wicked!" shouted the leader.

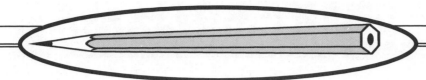

Rewrite these sentences using **capital letters, commas, full stops, question marks** or **exclamation marks.**

1. the explorer crossed deserts mountains oceans rivers glaciers and volcanoes

   _

2. he took with him camels to cross the desert canoes to cross rivers skis to cross the snow and climbing boots to scale the rocky mountains

   _

   _

3. he found rare flowers birds fish insects and animals

   _

4. the explorer faced all sorts of dangers: sharks crocodiles lions tigers mosquitoes snakes and bears

   _

   _

5. when the train stopped they could see the river thames in the distance

   _

6. if it is raining we will go to the london aquarium

   _

7. although it was getting dark we went on the great wheel of the london eye

   _

   _

8. look john you will have to go

   _

9. you fool you have let the fox into the chicken run

   _

10. shall i pass it to you samia

   _

Write down your score out of 10:

———
10

When you have got this page fully correct colour in the star.

39

commas & semi-colons

commas

❧ **Commas are used with words or phrases which give more information about another word.**

For example: • Jimmy, the champion goal scorer, fell to the ground.

Inserting the comma after Jimmy allows us to describe who or what Jimmy was like, before completing the main sentence.

• Alfred, England's greatest king, fought the Vikings and eventually won.

❧ **A comma is used to introduce speech.**

For example: • The sorcerer shouted, "Stop at once!"

• The football fan cheered, "Goal!"

❧ *A common error!*

Do not use a comma as a full stop.

Where one sentence ends and another begins, there should be a **full stop** and not a **comma**.

For example: • The dragon rolled over. It had breathed its last.

Not: • The dragon rolled over, it had breathed its last.

semi-colons

The semi-colon is half-way between a comma and a full stop.

It can be used to separate sentences that are close in meaning, instead of a full stop.

For example: • He ran down the stairs; he reached the door; he opened it.

• There were one hundred soldiers outside the palace; there were twenty policeman inside the palace; the thief walked passed them all; he stole the valuable diamond from under their noses!

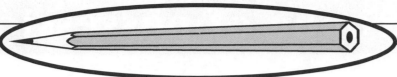
Rewrite these sentences using **capital letters**, **commas** where needed and **full stops**.

1.   the vikings the makers of fine long boats came from scandinavia

_ _

2.   the long boats fast and seaworthy travelled along the coast of britain

_ _

3.   the vikings no better than pirates attacked churches villages and towns near the sea _

_ _

4.   they even sailed up the rivers raiding killing and stealing right into gloucestershire the heart of the country _ _ _ _ _ _ _ _ _ _ _ _ _ _ _ _

_ _

_ _

5.   several kings brave and courageous battled with the vikings

_ _

6.   the general shouted we have won the battle

_ _

7.   what a beautiful smell sighed the tramp as he walked past the baker's shop

_ _

Semi-colons

Punctuate these following sentences.

8.   the ghost wailed sadly he rattled his ghostly chains he shook his gory fist he took off his head he disappeared from sight

_ _

_ _

9.   the night was clear the stars shone brightly it was very cold

_ _

Write down your score out of 9:

_____
9

When you have got this page fully correct colour in the star.

apostrophe of possession

This little mark is like a comma but always stands in line with the top of the letters – **9** . **Firstly it is used to show possession and secondly to show that letters have been missed out of a word.**

> showing possession

Firstly , it is used at the end of a word with an s, like this, **'s** .
It means *of* or *belonging to*.
For example: • The tree**'s** branches.
This has the same meaning as: *The branches of the tree*

  • the car**'s** wheel ...   the wheel of the car
  • the child**'s** doll ...   the doll of the child

If a word ends in an *s*, **the apostrophe can be placed after the s or with 's**

  • Jame**s'** or Jame**s's** head ...   the head of James
  • Franci**s'** or Franci**s's** coat ... the coat of Francis

When the apostrophe is placed before the s it is singular or one.

  • the tree**'s** branches ... the branches of the tree

When it comes after the final s it means plural or more than one.

  • the tree**s'** branches ... the branches of the trees
  • the car**s'** wheels ...   the wheels of the cars
  • the cow**s'** horns ...   the horns of the cows

There are certain words with **unusual plural forms** such as man *(men)*, child *(children)*, woman *(women)*, mouse *(mice)*. When using the plural form, the apostrophe is still placed as if it were singular, ie before the final *s*

  • the women**'s** hats ...   the hats of the women
  • the mice**'s** tails ...   the tails of the mice

A mistake to avoid:

Many people use the apostrophe to mean *lots of*:
*There were lots of sea shell**'s** on the shore.*
Wrong!

When a word indicates more than one it does not need an apostrophe.
There were lots of sea shells on the shore.
Right!

42

Change these **possessive words** into their longer form:
For example: • the river's bank ... **the bank of the river**

1.   the sun's light   _ _ _ _ _ _ _ _ _ _ _ _ _ _ _

2.   the earth's orbit   _ _ _ _ _ _ _ _ _ _ _ _ _ _ _

3.   the moon's pull   _ _ _ _ _ _ _ _ _ _ _ _ _ _ _

4.   the picture's frame   _ _ _ _ _ _ _ _ _ _ _ _ _ _ _

Change the following into the **possessive form:**
For example: • the blossom of the plant ... **the plant's blossom**

5.   the leg of the chair   _ _ _ _ _ _ _ _ _ _ _ _ _ _ _

6.   the handle of the cup   _ _ _ _ _ _ _ _ _ _ _ _ _ _ _

7.   the wheels of the car   _ _ _ _ _ _ _ _ _ _ _ _ _ _ _

8.   the wings of the aircraft   _ _ _ _ _ _ _ _ _ _ _ _ _ _

Change these **possessive words** into their longer form:
For example: • the cars' headlights ... **the headlights of the cars**

9.   the players' scores   _ _ _ _ _ _ _ _ _ _ _ _ _ _ _

10.   the horses' hooves   _ _ _ _ _ _ _ _ _ _ _ _ _ _

11.   the houses' roofs   _ _ _ _ _ _ _ _ _ _ _ _ _ _

12.   the birds' wings   _ _ _ _ _ _ _ _ _ _ _ _ _ _

Change the following into their **possessive form**:
For example: • the oars of the rowers ... **the rowers' oars**

13.   the engines of the jets   _ _ _ _ _ _ _ _ _ _ _ _ _ _

14.   the smoke of the chimneys   _ _ _ _ _ _ _ _ _ _ _ _ _ _

15.   the crash of the waves   _ _ _ _ _ _ _ _ _ _ _ _ _ _

Write down
your score
out of 15:

___
15

When you
have got this
page fully
correct colour
in the star.

43

Apostrophes: contractions

When we speak aloud we often run words together or shorten them. We do not often say, *"I cannot finish my homework; I should have started earlier."* We are more likely to say: *"I can't finish my homework; I should've started earlier!"* **Can't** is short for **can not** and **should've** is short for **should have**. We use an **apostrophe** to show that we have missed out some letters of the word.

Here is a list of some of the contractions in common use:

don't – do not   **won't** – will not   **isn't** – is not

I'll – I will   **you'll** – you will   **it's** – it is

I've – I have   **I'm** – I am   **he's** – he is or has

she'd – she had or would   **I'd** – I would or had

1. *I would've* is short for *I would have* not *I would of*!
2. *It's* is short for *It is* not *its,* the personal pronoun
For example: • The cat licked its paws. *(Correct)*
                        • The cat licked it's paws. *(Incorrect)*

A hint for writing
Only use the contraction when you are writing down speech directly. Only words inside the speech marks should be contracted.

Abbreviations using full stops

Sometimes we like to think of the easiest and quickest way of saying something and so we make certain words or collections of words as short as possible. Here are examples of abbreviations:

U.S.A. – The United States of America. **Rd.** – Road

A.A. – The Automobile Association   **Dr.** – Doctor

A.D. – in the year of Our Lord   **C.O.** – Commanding Officer

R.A.F. – The Royal Air Force   **H.M.S.** – Her Majesty's Ship

A.M.– Ante Meridien(before noon)

P.M. – Post Meridien(after noon)

Some abbreviations take the first letter and the last letter of a word to be shortened, for example *Doctor* becomes *Dr.* and *Mister* becomes *Mr.* Also *Road* becomes *Rd.* and *Street* becomes *St.*

> **Tip!**
> If you want to be really correct you should put a full stop after the letters showing the abbreviation. Often, however, the full stops are left out.

What do these mean when they are **not contracted by the apostrophe**?

1. didn't _ _ **did not** _ _

4. she's _ _ _ _ _ _ _ _ _ _

2. he'd _ _ _ _ _ _ _ _ _

5. he'll _ _ _ _ _ _ _ _ _

3. you'd _ _ _ _ _ _ _ _ _

6. you've _ _ _ _ _ _ _ _ _

In these sentences **contract** the two words in bold type by **adding the apostrophe**:

7. **He will** have to clean his room. _

8. They said **they would** come. _

9. I **shall not** forget. _

10. You **can not** stop now. _

Write down the **abbreviations** of the words in bold print. The first letter of the shortened word is usually a capital.

11. The **police constable** was from the **Criminal Investigation Department**. _ _ _ _ _ _ _ _

12. I posted the letter at the **general post office**. _ _ _ _

13. She likes to give money to the **National Society for the Prevention of Cruelty to Children** but he donates money to the **Royal Society for the Prevention of Cruelty to Animals**. _ _ _ _ _ _ _ _

14. Go **north east** and then **south west** until you reach the **head quarters** of the **commanding officer**. _ _ _ _ _ _ _ _ _ _ _ _ _ _ _ _

Here is a message. Write it in full:

15. Prof. Snell and Dr. Lamb arr. 11a.m. Mon. at Lndn. Airport or on Sat. 8th Mar. at 2pm Gtwk.

_ _

_ _

Write down your score out of 15:

_____

15

When you have got this page fully correct colour in the star.

45

direct speech

When you write down the actual words that someone speaks, it is called **direct speech** and those words need to be enclosed in speech marks. There are opening and closing speech marks which look like this: **66   99**

They **enclose the spoken words** and are written at the same height as the top of the letters. They are like **66** and **99** with the circles filled in.

For example: • "It will rain today."

The words *It will rain today* **are placed in speech marks to show that they have been spoken.**

> • The weather forecaster said, "It will rain today."

Note:

In grammatical language the word *said* is the *verb of saying*.

The person who is speaking is the subject of the verb and what is spoken is the object of the verb *said*. We will call the subject and the verb of saying, (the weather forecaster said,) the **speech introduction**.

There are **three most common patterns of speech**.

first pattern

♦ The first pattern of direct speech

CL _ _ _ _ _ , " CL _ _ _ _ _ ." (*CL* stands for Capital letter)

For example: • The policeman said, "The telephone is ringing."

The speech introduction *(The policeman said)* **comes before the words of speech** *(The telephone is ringing)* and is followed by a comma, opening speech marks and a capital letter. It ends with a full stop and then the closing speech marks. Be very careful to keep to the order of the marks.

second pattern

♦ The second pattern of direct speech

" CL _ _ _ _ _ ," sl _ _ _ _ _ , (*sl* stands for small letter)

For example: • "The telephone is ringing," said the policeman.

The words of speech *(The telephone is ringing)* **begin with opening speech marks and a capital letter and end with a comma and closing speech marks, and are followed by the speech introduction** *(said the policeman)* starting with a small letter and ending with a full stop.

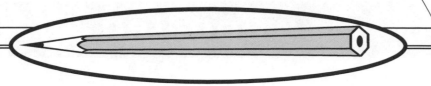

The first pattern of direct speech

Re-write these sentences using **capital letters, commas, speech marks** & **full stops, question marks or exclamation marks**.

1.　　sally looked out of the window and said it's snowing

　　－－－－－－－－－－－－－－－－－－－－－－－－－－－－－－－

2.　　john exclaimed it must be about six inches deep

　　－－－－－－－－－－－－－－－－－－－－－－－－－－－－－－－

3.　　they shouted mum can we go and play in the park

　　－－－－－－－－－－－－－－－－－－－－－－－－－－－－－－－

4.　　mrs smith replied yes you can but dress up warmly

　　－－－－－－－－－－－－－－－－－－－－－－－－－－－－－－－

There are five words **introducing speech** in these sentences. What are they?

5.　　－－－－－－－　　6.　　－－－－－－－　　7.　　－－－－－－－

8.　　－－－－－－－

The second pattern of direct speech

Re-write these sentences using **capital letters, commas, speech marks, full stops** or **exclamation marks**.

9.　　it's snowing cursed mr smith looking out of the window

　　－－－－－－－－－－－－－－－－－－－－－－－－－－－－－－－

10.　　the roads will be slippery he muttered under his breath

　　－－－－－－－－－－－－－－－－－－－－－－－－－－－－－－－

11.　　no one will get up the hill added mrs smith grimly

　　－－－－－－－－－－－－－－－－－－－－－－－－－－－－－－－

12.　　the trains will be late too stated mr smith

　　－－－－－－－－－－－－－－－－－－－－－－－－－－－－－－－

13.　　what a day it s going to be they declared together

　　－－－－－－－－－－－－－－－－－－－－－－－－－－－－－－－

There are five words **introducing speech** in these sentences. What are they?

14.　　－－－－－－－　　15.　　－－－－－－－　　16.　　－－－－－－－

17.　　－－－－－－－　　18.　　－－－－－－－

Write down your score out of 18:

－－－－－

18

When you have got this page fully correct colour in the star.

❧ The third pattern of direct speech

"*CL* _ _ _ _ _ ," *sl* _ _ _ _ _ , "*sl* _ _ _ _ _ ."
(*CL* stands for Capital letter, *sl* stands for small letter)

The third pattern of speech is shown when **a sentence is interrupted to put in the speech introduction.**

For example • "It's snowing," muttered Mr Smith, "and blizzards are on the way."
  • "I cannot remember," said Mrs Smith, "a worse year for terrible weather!"

There are thirteen basic steps:

1. opening speech marks
2. capital letter
3. words of direct speech
4. comma
5. closing speech marks
6. small letter
   (unless it's a name)
7. words of speech introduction
8. comma
9. opening speech marks
10. small letter (unless it's a name)
11. words of direct speech continued
12. full stop
13. closing speech marks.

❧ Writing conversations

Writing down conversations follows all the previous rules and patterns. There is one major rule which is this:

Whenever there is a change of speaker, begin on a new line with an indentation.
An indentation is a small space about the width of your first finger left at the beginning of the line.

For example: •   "Where did you put my book?" asked Simon.
    "I haven't moved it," replied Mark.
     Simon thought for a moment and then said, "I must have left it in the garden. I was reading it there."
      "It'll be covered in dew if it's been there all night!" stated Mark.

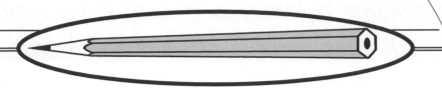

The third pattern of direct speech

Punctuate these sentences following all the rules given opposite. Use the examples opposite as guides.

1. temperatures announced the weather forecaster brightly will rise quickly tonight

   _

2. that means said mr smith with a sigh of relief that i can get to work without a three hour journey

   _

3. by tomorrow wailed the children all the snow will have gone

   _

Writing conversations

Punctuate these **conversations**. Do not forget the rule: Whenever there is a change in speaker, start a new line with an indentation.

4. what time is it it's four o'clock   _ _ _ _ _ _ _ _ _ _ _ _ _ _ _ _ _

   _ _ _ _ _ _ _ _ _ _ _ _ _ _ _ _ _

5. did you see that car asked the policeman it was a porsche and going very fast replied hamish

   _

   _

6. do you know what happened to the old man asked the ambulance paramedic he was not looking where he was going replied joanna and he slipped and fell

   _

   _

   _

Write down your score out of 6:

_____
6

When you have got this page fully correct colour in the star.

colons, dashes, brackets

colons

Colons are used to introduce a list especially after words such as, *as follows* or *the following* .

For example: • When you travel to France, you will need the
following:
a bathing suit
a towel
a pair of short trousers for the beach
a track suit
a pair of running shoes

• There are two reasons why you should not go to
the party: you have not finished your work and
you have not cleaned the oil off your clothes.

dashes

We often want to add more information to or comment on our sentences. There are two ways that extra information or information 'on the side' can be added in.
Firstly, **dashes**, short horizontal lines like this: –
These are for extra comments on the sentence.

For example: • Professor Knight sneezed – it was a terrible noise
which resounded round the room – and then
continued his lecture.
• They say that the piercing sound of trumpets –
highly tuned and blown closely together – could
cause the wall to shake and fall.

brackets

Secondly , **brackets *for adding extra information.***
Brackets are always in pairs : **(   )**

For example: • Go straight to the hall **(**third large door on the left**)**.
• Queen Victoria **(**1837 -1901**)** was one of the longest
reigning monarchs this country has ever known.

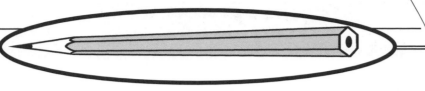

Punctuate these Sentences:

Colons

1.   bring the following three apples four pears six bananas

   _

   _

2.   the explorer had two aims in mind to discover the lost tribe of matazoo
   to find the great pearl of queen natanga

   _

   _

Dashes

3.   professor nuthead professor nutty would be a better name searched for
   the glasses that were already on the tip of his nose

   _

   _

4.   the whole basket and its contents eggs milk jars of honey treacle
   toppled onto the floor

   _

   _

Brackets

5.   It was strange: he was born in boston england but lived in boston usa

   _

   _

6.   the great general Born 1765–Died 1827 fought many great battles

   _

   _

Write down
your score
out of 6:

_____
6

When you
have got this
page fully
correct colour
in the star.

setting out letters

A well set out letter is always a joy to see, whether it is a letter from a friend or an acquaintance or a business letter. It is worthwhile taking proper care to write neatly with a correctly laid out address.

Rules for heading a letter

1. Your address goes on the first line starting towards the right of the page:

2. The name of the district that you live in is written on the next line and a little to the right :

3. Name of the town or city. This is written on the next line down, again a little further to the right and with the postcode.

4. Leave a space and then write the date:

5. On the next line down on the other side of the page you start the letter with:

   Dear Aunt Jill and Uncle Michael,

6. Note that after the end of the name of the person to whom the letter is addressed, there is a comma. On the next line down, start the contents of your letter under the comma:

   Thank you very much for the gift you sent me at Christmas.

7. You will find that the contents of a letter may divide into three or four sections dealing with different subjects. Each of these sections or paragraphs should start on a new line with an indentation, that is, a finger's width in from the margin of the page.

8. At the end of the letter, on a new line, begin your closing greeting with an appropriate finish. There are many ways of closing but here are a few examples:

   a. To a close relative or dear friend, you might sign your letter:

   With love and best wishes,

   Martin.

   b. To a someone you know such as an adult or teacher:

   Your sincerely,

   c. To someone you do not know:

   Yours faithfully,

---

56 Stannard Rd,
Fulham,
London SW18 5TY

14th January 2001

Dear ......,

Thankyou...

With Love,

Note:

Note that the closing words are in the middle of the page after the contents of the letter.

Set out the following addresses as shown.

For example: Set out this address:
92 jesper road collingsbury sussex as 32 8jh 14th may 2001 dear dr jimson

> 92 Jesper Road,
> Collingsbury,
> Sussex AS32 8JH
>
> 14th May 2001

Dear Dr. Jimson,

1. 81 summerly gardens thurley oxfordshire ox2 5hy 22nd september 2001 dear mrs jode

   _____
   _____
   _____
   _____
   _____

   _____

2. 19 beaulieu crescent hampstead london nw11 6nm 25th june 2001 dear uncle philip thank you very much for the gift of £10 for christmas it was very kind of you i shall be passing through tonbridge on friday may I visit you then with much love timothy

   _____
   _____
   _____
   _____
   _____

   _____

   _____

   _____

   _____

53

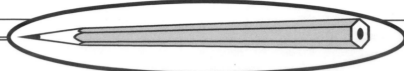

Revision

Write down the words which should begin with **capital letters** in these sentences:

1. shakespeare lived his early life at stratford, which is in warwickshire.

    _ _ _ _ _ _ _ _ _ _   _ _ _ _ _ _ _ _ _ _   _ _ _ _ _ _ _ _ _ _

2. snowdon is the highest mountain in wales.

    _ _ _ _ _ _ _ _ _ _   _ _ _ _ _ _ _ _ _ _

Punctuate these sentences using **capitals, commas** and **full stops** or **question** or **exclamation marks**:

3. please buy cabbages cauliflower carrots and potatoes

    _

4. simon got out of bed dressed came downstairs ate his breakfast and went

    to school. _

    _

5. when did sarah go shopping

    _

6. what a lovely dress

    _

Apostrophes of possession

Punctuate the following sentences with **apostrophes**, **capital letters** and **fullstops**:

7. the elephant s tusks and the bull s horns are powerful weapons

    _

8. the books pages were ruined by the fire in the library

    _

Apostrophes of contraction & abbreviations

Write these words in full:

9. you've _ _ _ _ _ _ _ _ _ _ _   11. shan't _ _ _ _ _ _ _ _ _ _

10. I've _ _ _ _ _ _ _ _ _ _   12. aren't _ _ _ _ _ _ _ _ _ _

Using **apostrophes**, contract these:

13. would have _ _ _ _ _ _ _ _ _ _   15. is not _ _ _ _ _ _ _ _ _ _ _

14. has not _ _ _ _ _ _ _ _ _ _   16. he would _ _ _ _ _ _ _ _ _

What are these short for?

17. R.A.F. _ _ _ _ _ _ _ _ _ _ _ _ _ _   19. Dr. _ _ _ _ _ _ _ _ _ _ _ _ _

18. H.M.S. _ _ _ _ _ _ _ _ _ _ _ _ _ _   20. U.K. _ _ _ _ _ _ _ _ _ _ _ _ _

Direct Speech

Punctuate these sentences using **capital letters**, **commas**, **apostrophes**, **speech marks** and **full stops**, **question marks** or **exclamation marks**:

21. jenny shouted whats going on

_ _

22. there's a ghost in here replied sandra

_ _

23. if there is a ghost stammered dominic i'm off

_ _

24. who let the secret out demanded don
    i dont know replied jack

_ _

_ _

Semi-colons, colons

Punctuate the following sentences:

25. she went into the kitchen she cooked supper she fed the baby she fell
    asleep in front of the fire

_ _

_ _

26. follow these instructions light the blue paper and stand well back

_ _

_ _

Write down
your score
out of 26:

_____
26

When you
have got this
page fully
correct colour
in the star.

Alphabetical order

Putting things in order helps to put our minds in order, and this helps us to think clearly. A dictionary puts words in the order of the alphabet. The alphabet gets its name from **alpha** and **beta**, the first two letters in Greek.

The alphabet is a marvellous system because it enables us to write all the words of the English language with just 26 letters:

There are 26 letters in our alphabet

a b c d e f g h i
j k l m n o p q r
s t u v w x y z

We usually divide the alphabet into two groups of letters: **vowels** and **consonants**.

vowels

The vowels are: **a e i o u**. They can be sounded by themselves.

consonants

The consonants are all the other letters. They need vowels to help them to sound.

putting in order

❥ If you are asked to put a group of words into alphabetical order, **the first letter of each word will usually tell you its position.**
So:
parrot, *dog*, *cat* and *mouse* will appear in alphabetical order as:
cat, *dog*, *mouse*, and *parrot*.

❥ **But if several words begin with the same letter you have to take the second letter into account.**
Thus *sugar*, *see*, *show*, and *sight* are put into alphabetical order as: *see*, *show*, *sight*, and *sugar*.

❥ You might even have to think about third letters, as with *this*, *that*, *the*, and *thyme*, which become:
that, *the*, *this*, and *thyme*.

1. Here are some school subjects.
   In the boxes re-write them in **alphabetical order.**

Science	English	Mathematics	History	Art

2. Put these colours into **alphabetical order**.

red	blue	yellow	black	green	orange

3. Put the days of the week into **alphabetical order.**
   Make sure you spell each one correctly!

Monday	Tuesday	Wednesday	Thursday	Friday	Saturday	Sunday

4. These words all begin with *th*. Arrange them **alphabetically**.

thought	think	those	these	there	thud	thank	thing	then

5. These words all begin with *s*. Arrange them **alphabetically**.

sugar	sweet	saviour	saint	sat	swing	switch	snake	snarl

Write down
your score
out of 5:

———
5

When you
have got this
page fully
correct colour
in the star.

57

Magic 'e'

Magic 'e' has the power to change the sound and meaning of a word. In fact, it produces a new word!

A silent *e* after one consonant opens up the syllable and makes the preceding vowel long.

A syllable is one 'sound beat' within a word

Monosyllables are words of one (mono) syllable.

cap is a monosyllable because it has just *one* vowel sound *(a)*. The *a* is a short vowel.

add 'e'

When Magic **'e'** appears at the end it produces *cape*. *cape* is still a monosyllable, but what a different sound and meaning it now has! The vowel *a* has now become long.

cap

cape

➤ **Note:** Remember that *e* is always silent at the end of words. If you hear the sound *e* use the letter *y*. e.g store but stor*y*.

Other examples of magic e are:

• pin	• **pine**
• hop	• **hope**
• cut	• **cute**
• her	• **here**
• glad	• **glade** *(forest)*
• mop	• **mope**
• tap	• **tape**
• plum	• **plume**

Let the magic 'e' work. Look at the word in the first column. Say the word to yourself. In the second column write the word with the **magic 'e'** at the end. Say this new word to yourself! In the third column see if you can write the meaning of the word with the magic 'e'. You can use a dictionary, or ask other people, if you want to.

	Word	Magic 'e' word	Meaning of word with magic E.
1.	bit	bite	Cut with your teeth
2.	spin		
3.	can		
4.	man		
5.	pan		
6.	kit		
7.	pip		
8.	fat		
9.	pal		
10.	win		
11.	twin		
12.	mad		
13.	not		
14.	fir		
15.	mat		

Choosing from the words in the brackets pick the correct word to make the sentences complete.

16. I felt a tingling down my _ _ _ _ _ _ _. (**spin/spine**)

17. Can I _ _ _ _ _ _ _ the wheel? (**spin/spine**)

18. Please _ _ _ _ _ _ _ down on this chair. (**sit/site**)

19. The building _ _ _ _ _ _ _ was particularly messy. (**sit/site**)

20. The _ _ _ _ _ _ _ is dripping. (**tap/tape**)

21. That was a good music _ _ _ _ _ _ _ . (**tap/tape**)

22. I've _ _ _ _ _ _ _ my finger. (**cut/cute**)

23. What a _ _ _ _ _ _ _ little kitten! (**cut/cute**)

Write down your score out of 23:

_____

23

When you have got this page fully correct colour in the star.

Special combinations

'qu' sounds like 'kw'

In English words the letter **q** is always followed by **u**, but the two letters together usually sound like **kw** when they come at the beginning of a word or in the middle of a word,

For example:

- **qu**een
- **qu**arter
- **qu**iet
- in**qu**est
- **qu**ickly
- **qu**est
- **qu**ite

Two special letters together sound like another letter

Another special combination is **ph**, which sounds like **f**.

'ph' sounds like 'f'

For example:

- **Ph**easant
- tele**ph**one
- **ph**antom
- **ph**armacy
- ne**ph**ew
- **ph**otogra**ph**
- **ph**ysics
- gra**ph**
- al**ph**abet

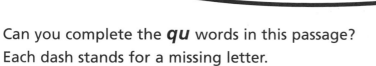

Can you complete the **qu** words in this passage?
Each dash stands for a missing letter.

| queues | questions | quoted | quake |

| quench | inquiry | quickly | quarter |

1. The earth **qu** _ _ _   destroyed a **qu** _ _ _ _ _   of the city, and long

qu _ _ _ _   **qu** _ _ _ _ _   formed at the relief centres. No **qu** _ _ _ _ _ _ _ _

were asked and fresh water was given to everyone to **qu** _ _ _ _   their thirst.

A figure of 300 dead was **qu** _ _ _ _   and a team of investigators began their

inqu _ _ _ .

Good. Now can you complete the **ph** words in the next passage?

| phenomenally | pharaohs | philosophers | physicians | sphinx | photographs |

2. The rulers of ancient Egypt were called **ph** _ _ _ _ _ _ . Many were priests and

some were also **ph** _ _ _ _ _ **ph** _ _ _   and **ph** _ _ _ _ _ _ _ _ _. Reports and

ph _ _ _ _ _ _ **ph** _ of their tombs show how **ph** _ _ _ _ _ _ _ _ _ _   wealthy

they must have been. One of the great mysteries is that of the _ **ph** _ _ _ ,

a huge statue looking like a lion with a human face.

Write down
your score
out of 2:

———
2

When you
have got this
page fully
correct colour
in the star.

61

Sounds the same

Sometimes two words sound the same, but their spellings are different and they have different meanings. Such words are called **homophones (homo – the same, phones – sounds).**

> 'homo' = the same
> 'phones' = sounds

So when you are trying to find a **homophone**, the secret is to listen carefully to the word you have been given, and your mind will tell you if you know another word with the same sound.

For example, if you hear the sound of the word *hair*, your mind may first give you a picture such as:

hair

> same sound

But if you listen to the same sound once or twice more, you may now have a mental picture of:

hare

Other homophones:

- witch
- stare
- son
- hour
- meddle
- deer

- which
- stair
- sun
- our
- medal
- dear

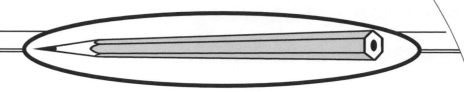

By listening to the sound of each word in the first column, see if you can get a mental picture of the **homophone**. Write the homophone in the second column and try to write its meaning. You can use a dictionary, or ask other people to help you, if you want to. The first one is done for you.

	Word	Homophone	Meaning of Homophone
1.	In	Inn	Kind of hotel or pub.
2.	flower		
3.	pale		
4.	not		
5.	hear		
6.	bare		
7.	bred		
8.	tire		
9.	tee		
10.	our		
11.	heel		

Choose a word from those in brackets to complete the sentences.

12. We made sand castles at the _ _ _ _ _ _ _ today. **(beech/beach)**

13. My train _ _ _ _ _ _ _ was very expensive. **(fare/fair)**

14. Vegetarians do not eat _ _ _ _ _ _ _. **(meet/meat)**

15. I _ _ _ _ _ _ _ a small donkey. **(road/rode)**

16. _ _ _ _ _ _ _ you like a cup of tea? **(would/wood)**

Join the words that sound the same:

17. **heir** **week**

18. **die** **by**

19. **ate** **air**

20. **buy** **eight**

21. **weak** **dye**

Write down your score out of 21:

———
21

When you have got this page fully correct colour in the star.

63

Identical twins

Sometimes you find two words with the **same sound and the same spelling,** but their **meanings are different.**

They look the same and they sound the same → **These words are called *homonyms***

The word ***port*** is a good example. We can say that the ship sailed slowly into ***port*** (harbour).

And we can talk about an old man enjoying his glass of ***port*** (alcoholic drink).

The word ***arms*** is another example. Thus, the gorilla has long ***arms.***

But we can also talk of the terrorists who were ordered to lay down their ***arms*** (weapons).

- A word can also have many different meanings. This is where a dictionary becomes extremely useful.

Other homonyms:

- iron (ironing)
- jumper (clothes)
- present (gift)
- will (resolve)

- iron (metal)
- jumper (verb: to jump)
- present (here, now)
- will (legacy)

Now let's see if you can identify the **identical twins** in the following sentences. Each dash represents one missing letter.

Tip: It usually helps to look at two sentences together in order to find your answers.

1. a The cashier put the money into the _ _ _ _ .

   b I waited _ _ _ _ the teacher called me.

2. a In autumn the _ _ _ _ _ _ on most trees turn brown.

   b My sister _ _ _ _ _ _ at seven every morning.

3. a King Alfred was one of the greatest English _ _ _ _ _ _ _ .

   b We were asked to underline the title with our _ _ _ _ _ _ .

4. a The prisoners refused to eat. They were going to _ _ _ _ until they died.

   b It is an offense to drive too _ _ _ _ .

5. a Take the second turning on the _ _ _ _ .

   b The safe was empty. There was nothing _ _ _ _ .

6. a Put the dirty cutlery in the washing-up _ _ _ _ .

   b At cricket practice they took it in turns to _ _ _ _ .

The word **note** has many different meanings.
For example: a Something written down to help the memory.

b A short letter or written message.

c In music, a single sound of a particular pitch.

d A quality, a sound, a tone.

e Paper money.

Here are five sentences all containing the word **note**. Which meaning given above matches the sentences below? Write the letter of the matching meaning after the sentence.

7. He played the note Middle C on the piano. _ _c _ _

8. There was a note of anger in his voice. _ _ _ _

9. He left me a short note on the kitchen table. _ _ _ _

10. He passed the beggar a five pound note. _ _ _ _

11. He made a note of the telephone number. _ _ _ _

Write down
your score
out of II:

_____
II

When you
have got this
page fully
correct colour
in the star.

65

'i' before 'e'

❧ **There is a general rule that 'i' comes before 'e' in a word except after 'c' .**

'i' before 'e' except after 'c'

The winning team re**cei**ves a sh**ie**ld.

- ch**ie**f • br**ie**f • rel**ie**ve • bel**ie**f • p**ie**ce • gr**ie**f
- exper**ie**nce • v**ie**w • al**ie**n • pat**ie**nt • t**ie**
- n**ie**ce • pr**ie**st • fr**ie**ze

❧ **After a 'c' in a word, 'e' is written before 'i':**

- c**ei**ling • rec**ei**pt • rec**ei**ve • perc**ei**ve • dec**ei**t

❧ Although this is a good rule, there are some exceptions, the most important of which are:

exceptions

- th**ei**r • **ei**ther • n**ei**ther • forf**ei**t • s**ei**zed • spec**ie**s

- Their n**ie**ce discovered a new spec**ie**s of flower which neither of them knew about.

Here are other exceptions to the rule:
- w**ei**gh • n**ei**ghbour • r**ei**n • v**ei**n • **ei**ght • v**ei**l

You will notice that in these last exceptions the letters *ei* together make the sound of *ai*. Use this as a guideline to help you spot exceptions to this rule.

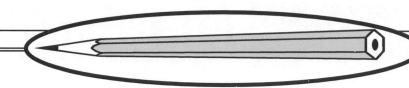

Add *i* and *e* to the following words.
Make sure they are in the correct order each time! To help you, the exceptions to the rule are marked with a *.

1.   p _ _ ce

2.   f _ _ ld

3.   dec _ _ ve

4.   th _ _ f

5.   fr _ _ nd

6.   rel _ _ f

7.   misch _ _ vous

8.   shr _ _ k

9.   sh _ _ ld

10. bel _ _ f

11. pat _ _ nt

12. s _ _ ge

13. ch _ _ f

14. y _ _ ld

15. r _ _ n *

16. h _ _ ght *

17. w _ _ ght *

18. s _ _ ve

19. ach _ _ ve

20. v _ _ w

21. d _ _ sel

22. gr _ _ f

23. c _ _ ling

24. _ _ ght *

25. v _ _ l *

26. sl _ _ gh *

27. n _ _ ghbour *

28. pr _ _ st

29. s _ _ ze *

30. prot _ _ n *

31. r _ _ gn *

32. fr _ _ ze

33. al _ _ n

34. med _ _ val

35. exper _ _ nce

36. ser _ _ s

37. t _ _

38. qu _ _ t

39. t _ _ r

40. perc _ _ ve

Write down your score out of 40:

———
40

When you have got this page fully correct colour in the star.

To double or not to double

We often have to think very carefully whether consonants should be double or single.

There is a rule about double consonants in the middle of a word.

to double

❯ **After a short vowel sound (where a word ends in *er*, *ing*, *on*, or *ed*,) a consonant is doubled.**

For example:
• ma**nn**er • se**tt**ing • fi**ll**ing • co**mm**on • fu**ll**er • fi**ll**ed

not to double

❯ **After a long vowel or if there are two vowels together one consonant is usually enough.**

For example:
• ba**b**y • fee**l**ing • ti**l**ing • moa**n**ing • fu**m**ing

If we double a consonant in the wrong place or use a single instead of a double we can change dramatically the meaning of a word. The sentence might end up not making sense.

For example:

• The girl fi**l**ed her finger nails. *(correct)*
• The girl fi**ll**ed her finger nails. *(incorrect)*

• The girl fi**ll**ed the jug with water. *(correct)*
• The girl fi**l**ed the jug of water. *(incorrect)*

• diner	• dinner
• holy	• holly
• staring	• starring
• below	• bellow
• pined	• pinned

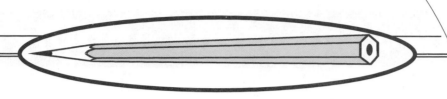

Circle the correct word.

1.	a vegetable	**cabage**	**cabbage**
2.	a vehicle	**lory**	**lorry**
3.	underneath	**below**	**bellow**
4.	land of sand	**desert**	**dessert**
5.	sweet course	**desert**	**dessert**
6.	root vegetable	**carot**	**carrot**
7.	colour	**redish**	**reddish**
8.	rabbits love it	**letuce**	**lettuce**
9.	not the same	**diferent**	**different**
10.	tool	**hamer**	**hammer**
11.	finished	**completed**	**completted**
12.	stayed	**remained**	**remainned**
13.	frothing	**foaming**	**foamming**
14.	provide food	**cater**	**catter**
15.	part of a word	**sylable**	**syllable**

16. I love that new bicycle you're **riding/ridding**.
17. What would you like to eat for **diner/dinner**?
18. We had fish and chips for **super/supper**.
19. Alice got very confused at the tea-party given by the mad **hater/hatter**.
20. I have to go to the dentist for a **filing/filling**.
21. My nails are too long. They need **filing/filling**.
22. The kitchen floor needs **moping/mopping**.
23. This new computer game is absolutely **super/supper**.
24. At Christmas we decorated the house with **holy/holly**.
25. Every Friday the flour was carted to market by the local **miler/miller**.
26. The blackberries are sour. Wait until they are **riper/ripper**.
27. Does anyone know the identity of Jack the **Riper/Ripper**?
28. Sweet-smelling curls of mahogany fell from the wood the carpenter was **planing/planning**.
29. Annabelle won the competition for the **boniest/bonniest** baby.
30. This is a new film in which my favourite actor is **staring/starring**.

Write down your score out of 30:

———

30

When you have got this page fully correct colour in the star.

Choose the right ending

At the end of many words there are five different spellings which sound very similar when you say them, and many people need help in choosing the right spelling.

The five endings are: **er**, **or**, **ar**, **our** and **re**.

Here are some tips (not rules) to help you choose the right one

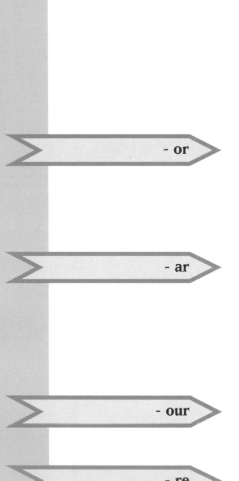

- er
> ❥ **er** is the most usual. It is used for many (but not all!) **occupations** e.g. • lecturer • baker
> ❥ for **comparative adjectives** e.g. • better • nicer
> ❥ an **inhabitant** e.g • Londoner • New Yorker

Many words ending in **er** are short simple words of everyday living.
For example: • sister • elder • rubber • summer • printer

- or
> ❥ **or** is used at the end of words when the **root ends** in **ct, it, ate** or **ess**
> *For example* • investigator • editor • tractor • inspector
> • possessor • exhibitor • assessor

- ar
> ❥ **ar** is used in an **adjective** when it means *like*
> *For example* • angular • circular
> ❥ used at the end of words, often after a single or double **l**
> *For example* • solar • polar • collar • cellar • pillar

- our
> ❥ **our** often ends an **abstract noun**
> *For example* • vigour • ardour • odour

- re
> ❥ **re** is used for **measurement units**
> *For example* • metre • litre • kilometre

If you cannot spell it then look it up

Remember: if you are not sure how to spell a word, it is no disgrace to use a dictionary or ask for help. In fact, it is an intelligent approach.

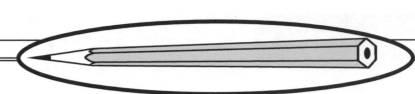

er   or   ar   our   re

Add the right endings to these words.

1.   **rectangul** _____

2.   **doll** _____

3.   **fibb** _____

4.   **doct** _____

5.   **farm** _____

6.   **behavi** _____

7.   **lawy** _____

8.   **cell** _____

9.   **met** _____

10. **triangul** _____

11. **pill** _____

12. **helicopt** _____

13. **photograph** _____

14. **spectat** _____

15. **butch** _____

16. **tract** _____

17. **coll** _____

18. **light** _____

19. **hum** _____

20. **litt** _____

21. **sist** _____

22. **broth** _____

23. **centimet** _____

24. **creat** _____

25. **slow** _____

26. **great** _____

27. **edit** _____

28. **busi** _____

29. **vig** _____

30. **charact** _____

31. **particul** _____

32. **lit** _____

33. **matt** _____

34. **moth** _____

35. **glam** _____

36. **assess** _____

37. **don** _____

38. **regul** _____

39. **murder** _____

40. **view** _____

Write down your score out of 40:

_____
40

When you have got this page fully correct colour in the star.

-le, -el, -al

le, el and *al* are endings which are often confused because they sound alike.

-le

❧ When you hear the *l* sound at the end of a multisyllable word, use *le* if the letter before the *l* sound has a stick or tail.

e.g • enjoyab**le** • thimb**le** • raff**le** • reasonab**le**
  • bund**le** • sadd**le** • lad**le** • fab**le** • app**le**

❧ Use *le* to keep *c* and *g* **hard**.

e.g • icic**le** • vehic**le** • ang**le** • obstac**le** • bung**le**

-el

❧ Use *el* to keep *c* and *g* **soft**.

e.g. • ang**el** • canc**el** • parc**el**

Use *el* if the letter before the *l* sound has **no stick or tail**.

e.g • tow**el** • shov**el** • trav**el** • nov**el**

-al

❧ Use *al* for adjectives

e.g. • leg**al** • magic**al** • tot**al** • physic**al** • spheric**al**

Use *al* when there is a whole word before the *l* sound.

• magic ⟶ • magic**al**

• music ⟶ • music**al**

• mechanic ⟶ • mechanic**al**

• fiction ⟶ • fiction**al**

• nation ⟶ • nation**al**

Add the correct endings by choosing between *le*, *el* and *al*.

1.	**electric** _ _	21.	**enjoyab** _ _
2.	**icic** _ _	22.	**spheric** _ _
3.	**season** _ _	23.	**obstac** _ _
4.	**knuck** _ _	24.	**mechanic** _ _
5.	**edib** _ _	25.	**feeb** _ _
6.	**canc** _ _	26.	**tow** _ _
7.	**reasonab** _ _	27.	**thimb** _ _
8.	**critic** _ _	28	**sadd** _ _
9.	**artic** _ _	29.	**tot** _ _
10.	**partic** _ _	30.	**inflatab** _ _
11.	**indecipherab** _ _	31.	**technic** _ _
12.	**vehic** _ _	32.	**horizont** _ _
13.	**fab** _ _	33.	**leg** _ _
14.	**fiction** _ _	34.	**lad** _ _
15.	**cubic** _ _	35.	**leth** _ _
16.	**physic** _ _	36.	**lev** _ _
17.	**parc** _ _	37.	**trav** _ _
18.	**mirac** _ _	38.	**shov** _ _
19.	**fin** _ _	39.	**brut** _ _
20.	**flammab** _ _	40.	**anim** _ _

Write down your score out of 40:

———
40

When you have got this page fully correct colour in the star.

Atten-shun!

Many English nouns end with the sound -*shun*, which can be spelt in different ways.

By far the most common spelling for this ending is -*tion*,

-tion

❯ Use -*tion* at the end of a word if the word ends in the sound *t*.

- act
- action
- relate
- relation
- dissect
- dissection

❯ Use -*tion* if the sound comes after a long vowel.
- combination • vacation • completion • potion

❯ Use -*tion* immediately after a short *i*.
- perdition • definition • condition

-sion

❯ Nouns with the ending -*sion* usually come from verbs with the endings *nd, ge, vert* and *pel*.

- apprehend
- apprehension
- submerge
- submersion
- divert
- diversion
- compel
- compulsion

-ssion

❯ Use -*ssion* when the baseword ends in *ss*.

- digress
- digression
- confess
- confession

❯ Nouns with the ending -*ssion* usually come from verbs ending with the root *mit, cede* or *ceed*.

- permit
- permission
- concede
- concession
- proceed
- procession

-cian

❯ Use -*cian* when referring to people.

- magic
- magician
- music
- musician
- politics
- politician

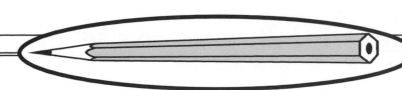

Now make your choice between **-tion**, **-sion**, **-ssion** and **-cian** to complete these nouns correctly.

1. **punctua**_____

2. **electri**_____

3. **associa** _____

4. **exclama** _____

5. **posse** _____

6. **posi** _____

7. **sess** _____

8. **sect** _____

9. **sedi** _____

10. **politi** _____

11. **quota** _____

12. **libera**_____

13. **na** _____

14. **ten** _____

15. **atten** _____

16. **confe** _____

17. **man** _____

18. **sta** _____

19. **recep**_____

20. **mi** _____

21. **perdi** _____

22. **musi** _____

23. **modera** _____

24. **physi** _____

25. **omi** _____

26. **occupa** _____

27. **obstruc** _____

28. **observa** _____

29. **pa** _____

30. **mathemati** _____

31. **peti**_____

32. **situa** _____

33. **medita** _____

34. **preven** _____

35. **depriva**_____

36. **deten** _____

37. **qualifica** _____

38. **conce**_____

39. **diver** _____

40. **combina** _____

Write down your score out of 40:

____
40

When you have got this page fully correct colour in the star.

75

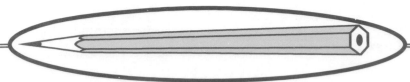

Revision

Alphabetical order

Arrange these animals in alphabetical order:

1. husky   horse   hog   hyena
    monkey   mink   mongoose

    _ _ _ _ _ _ _ _ _ _ _ _ _ _ _ _

    _ _ _ _ _ _ _ _ _ _ _ _ _ _

    _ _ _ _ _ _ _ _ _ _ _ _ _ _ _

Magic 'e'

Each of these words has a magic **e**. Say this word to yourself. Remove the magic **e** and say the new word. Write the meaning of the new word in the space provided.

2. made

    _ _ _ _ _ _ _ _ _

3. fine

    _ _ _ _ _ _ _ _ _

4. dine

    _ _ _ _ _ _ _ _ _

Homophones

Can you identify these homophones? Each dash represents one missing letter.

5. The bride walked gracefully
    up the _ _ _ _ _ .

    The castaways lived on a
    windswept _ _ _ _ .

6. Eating in the library is not

    _ _ _ _ _ _ _ .

    I'm not talking to myself. I'm
    just thinking _ _ _ _ _ .

7. The referee _ _ _ _ his whistle.

    The Union Jack is red, white
    and _ _ _ _ .

Special combinations

Complete the **qu** words. Each dash stands for a missing letter.

8. The boat was moored to the
    qu_ _ for a qu_ _ _ _ of an
    hour. The ducks started
    qu _ _ _ _ _ _ , the crew started
    qu _ _ _ _ _ _ _ _ _ , and the
    captain decided to qu_ _.

9. Now complete the **ph** words.
    Again, each dash represents a
    missing letter.

    Ph_ _ _ _ decided to study _ _ _ _ _
    _ _ _ ph_ _ _ so that he could read
    the language of the ancient
    Egyptians, but it gave him a
    headache, and so he asked the
    ph_ _ _ _ _ _ _ for some aspirins.
    The next day he felt better and he
    used his mobile ph_ _ _ to ask his
    friend about the ph_ _ _ _ _
    homework.

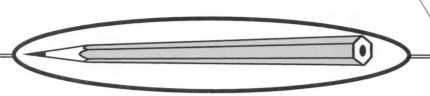

Rule for 'ie' and 'ei'

Add *ie* or *ei*, whichever is correct.

10.   rec _ _ ve
11.   p _ _ rce
12.   _ _ ther

13.   fr _ _ nd
14.   ch _ _ f
15.   conc _ _ ted

To double or not to double

Circle the correct spelling of the meaning of the bold words:

16.   **receive:**   accept   acept
17.   **helped:**   aidded   aided
18.   **recording:**   tapping   taping
19.   **necessary:**   essential   esential
20.   **smoking:**   fumming   fuming
21.   **a mistake:**   error   eror

Choose the right ending

-er, *-or*, *-ar*, *-our*, *-re*. Add the correct ending.

22.   support _ _
23.   mete _ _
24.   met _ _

25.   flav _ _ _
26.   vict _ _
27.   lun _ _

-al, *-le*. Add the correct ending.

28.   music _ _
29.   musc _ _
30.   leg _ _

31.   phenomen _ _
32.   thimb _ _
33.   tumb _ _

-tion, *-sion*. Add the correct ending.

34.   na _ _ _ _
35.   decep _ _ _ _
36.   ten _ _ _ _

37.   nega _ _ _ _
38.   affirma _ _ _ _
39.   deci _ _ _ _

Write down
your score
out of 39:

_____
39

When you
have got this
page fully
correct colour
in the star.

77

Answers

Grammar

Test 1
1. incomplete 2. complete 3. complete
4. incomplete
5. complete 6. ? 7. . 8. !
9. . . 10. . ? 11. !
12. and 13. or 14. but
15. because 16. if
17. when 18. although

Test 2
1. book, desk 2. mother, artist 3. elephants, ears
4. bus, theatre
5. concert, excitement
6. nurse, finger
7. teacher 8. party
9. garden 10. ducks
11. shock 12. Egypt
13. Robert 14. January
15. Paris 16. Spanish
17. **common nouns:** girl, birthday, city, iron
18. **Proper nouns:** Sarah, Monday, Paris, Eiffel Tower,

Test 3
1. pride 2. herd
3. crowd 4. plague
5. shoal 6. gang
7. string 8. cluster
9. love 10. jealousy
11. stillness
12. foot 13. rain
14. brush 15. John
16. shoal 17. peace, quietness, happiness
18. river, fish, rocks
19. towpath

Test 4
1. hands 2. chips
3. gloves 4. sisters
5. pens 6. Greeks
7. girls 8. children
9. beaches 10. feet
11. men 12. pupils
13. ladies 14. flies
15. wolves 16. sheep
17. mice 18. knives
19. fish 20. halves
21. deer 22. babies
23. teeth 24. women

Test 5
1. goes, present 2. will write, future 3. was, past 4. will fly, future
5. are, present
6. stayed, past
7. jogged 8. baked
9. were 10. looked
11. sang 12. lived
13. will cook 14. will play 15. will sing
16. will dance 17. will tidy 18. went 19. feel
20. will be 21. walked
22. played or was playing 23. left 24. is

Test 6
1. broke, active 2. was broken, passive 3. is being painted, passive
4. paints, active 5. sang, active 6. was sung, passive 7. was stolen, passive 8. will swim, active 9. The mouse was chased by the cat.
10. This book was written by Roald Dahl.
11. My sweater was knitted by my Gran.
12. This song was recorded by Robbie Williams. 13. The green team was beaten by the red team. 14. The winning car was driven by David Coulthard.
15. The teacher was helped by Jasmine and Sam. 16. The house will be completed by the builders tomorrow.

Test 7
1. has 2. am 3. do
4. will 5. was 6. has
7. do 8. can 9. may/can
10. could (or may or can) 11. must 12. might (or may) 13. ought
14. should 15. a. go
b. will 16. a. listened
b. had 17. a. to dress
b. ought 18. a. be b. will
19. a. learn b. must

Test 8
1. yes 2. yes 3. no
4. no 5. v. takes s. Lauren

6. v. was taken s. the test 7. v. drink s. the girl
8. v. are s. computer games 9. v. love s. we
10. v. is s. rose
11. Melanie 12. me
13. a snowball fight
14. this picture 15. car
16. teeth 17. grow
18. plays 19. play
20. starts 21. are
22. go 23. is 24. has
25. are 26. comes

Test 9
1. they 2. she 3. it
4. I 5. it 6. them
7. mine 8. his 9. theirs
10. who 11. which
12. whom (or that)
13. I, they, us
14. mine, ours, theirs
15. who, which, that

Test 10
1. hot, cool 2. long, elderly 3. nervous, important 4. tired, sore 5. new, gorgeous
6. angry, naughty
7. smaller 8. more successful 9. most skilful
10. highest 11. most expensive 12. younger, youngest 13. very happy 14. rather hungry 15. easy to understand
16. surprisingly comfortable

Test 11
1. v. cut adv. carefully
2. v. was hurt adv. badly
3. v. answer adv. honestly 4. v. plays adv. superbly
5. brightly 6. angrily
7. warmly 8. quickly
9. tomorrow 10. now
11. never 12. outside
13. there 14. far 15. too
16. extremely

Test 12
1. to 2. for 3. at
4. beside 5. Here is a box in which you can keep your pencils.
6. For whom are you

searching? 7. I met the girl with whom I go to school. 8. Find a peg on which you can hang your coat.
9. but 10. and
11. when 12. or
13. but 14. because
15. until/when
16. while

Test 13
1. a 2. the 3. a 4. an
5. the 6. the 7. a 8. an
9. an 10. the
11. radiator 12. early night 13. police station
14. taxi 15. hour

Test 14
1. wagged
2. eat
3. sing
4. compound
5. simple
6. complex
7. noun: chocolate
   abstract: happiness
8. noun: flower
   abstract: beauty
9. noun:
   conversation
   abstract: illness
10. sandwiches
11. teeth
12. wives
13. past
14. future
15. present
16. cut, active
17. was scored, passive
18. was built, passive
19. will or must
20. have
21. must
22. can
23. who
24. them
25. yours
26. rougher, roughest
27. bigger, biggest
28. more wonderful, most wonderful
29. soon
30. sadly
31. everywhere
32. above
33. to
34. under

35. because
36. but
37. although
38. the
39. a
40. an

Punctuation

Test 15
1. aA cC fF gG lL eE oO tT sS jJ oO nN xX yY zZ bB dD qQ
2. Bb Cc Jj Uu Yy Rr Ii Mm Qq Hh Ff Kk
3. Jack and Sam went to London. 4. Jane and Samina went shopping in Oxford Street.
5. The Titanic was on its way from Liverpool to New York.
6. Cardiff is the capital of Wales; Edinburgh is the capital of Scotland; Paris is the capital of France and Madrid is the capital of Spain.

Test 16
1. The world is round like a ball. 2. The earth goes round the sun in a year. 3. The moon orbits the earth.
4. Compared to the sun the earth is a small speck. 5. Once... flat. They... Helios. He... morning. He... day. In... horizon.
6. Why... custard?
7. Where... came?
8. How... tell? 9. Will... raining? 10. What... was! 11. The... off.
12. It... down! 13. It... sky. 14. The Titanic... Atlantic. 15. What's happened? 16. We're... down!

Test 17
1. The... deserts, mountains, oceans, rivers, glaciers and volcanoes. 2. He... desert, canoes... rivers, skis... mountains.

3. He... flowers, birds, fish, insects and animals.
4. The... sharks, crocodiles, lions, tigers, mosquitoes, snakes and bears.
5. When... stopped, they... River Thames... distance.
6. If... raining, we... London Aquarium.
7. Although... dark, we... London Eye.
8. Look, John, you... go! 9. You fool, you have... run! 10. Shall I pass... you, Samia?

Test 18
1. The Vikings, the... boats, came from Scandinavia.
2. The long boats, fast and seaworthy, travelled... Britain.
3. The Vikings, no better than pirates, attacked churches, villages and towns near the sea.
4. They... raiding, killing and stealing... Gloucestershire, the... country.
5. Several kings, brave and courageous, battled... Vikings.
6. The general shouted, we... battle. 7. What... smell, sighed the tramp, as... shop.
8. The... sadly; he... chains; he... fist; he... head; he... sight. 9. The... clear; the... brightly; it... cold.

Test 19
1. the light of the sun   2. the orbit of the earth
3. the pull of the moon 4. the frame of the picture

5. the chair's leg
6. the cup's handle
7. the car's wheels
8. the aircraft's wings 9. the scores of the players
10. the hooves of the horses 11. the roofs of the houses
12. the wings of the birds 13. the jets' engines
14. the chimneys' smoke 15. the waves' crash

Test 20
1. did not 2. he had or he would
3. you had or you would 4. she has or is 5. he will
6. you have
7. he'll 8. they'd
9. shan't 10. can't
11. P.C. C.I.D.
12. G.P.O.
13. N.S.P.C.C. R.S.P.C.A
14. N.E. S.W. H.Q. C.O.
15. Professor Snell and Doctor Lamb will arrive at 11 ante meridien on Monday at London Airport or on Saturday 8th March at 2 post meridien at Gatwick.

Test 21
1. Sally... said, "It's snowing."
2. John exclaimed, "It... deep!"
3. They shouted, "Mum, can... park?"
4. Mrs. Smith replied, "Yes, you can, but... warmly." 5. said
6. exclaimed
7. shouted
8. replied
9. "It's snowing!" cursed Mr. Smith, looking... window.
10. "The roads... slippery,"he...

breath. 11. "No-one... hill," added Mrs. Smith grimly.
12. "The trains... late, too," stated Mr. Smith.
13. "What... be!" they declared together.
14. cursed
15. muttered
16. added
17. stated
18. declared

Test 22
1."Temperatures," announced... brightly, "will... tonight."
2."That means," said Mr. Smith... relief, "that I... journey."
3."By tomorrow," wailed the children, "all the... gone."
4."What time is it?"
  "It's four o'clock."
5."Did you... car?" asked the policeman.
  "It was a Porsche... fast," replied Hamish.
6."Do... man?" asked... paramedic.
  "He was... going," replied Joanna, "and he slipped and fell."

Test 23
1.Bring the following: three apples, four pears, six bananas.
2.The explorer... mind: to discover... matazoo; to find... Queen Natanga.
3.Professor Nuthead - Professor Nutty... name - searched... nose.
4. The... contents - eggs, milk, jars of

honey, treacle - toppled... floor.
5. It was strange: he... Boston (England),but ... in Boston (U.S.A).
6. The great general (Born 1765 - Died 1827) fought... battles.

Test 24
1. **1st line**: 81... Gardens,
2nd line: (indent) Thurley,
3rd line: (indent) Oxfordshire OX2 5HY
4th line: space
5th line: 22nd September 2001
6th line: (left of page) Dear Mrs. Jode
2. **1st line**: 19 Beaulieu Crescent,
2nd line: (indent) Hampstead,
3rd line: (indent) London NW11 6NM
4th line: space
5th line: 25th June 2001
6th line: (left of page) Dear Uncle Philip,
7th line: (paragraph indent) Thankyou... Christmas. It... you.
8th line: (paragraph indent) I... Tonebridge on Friday. May... then?
9th line: space
10th line: (paragraph indent) With... love,
11th line: Timothy

Test 25
1. Shakespeare Stratford Warwickshire.
2. Snowdon Wales.
3. Please buy cabbages, cauliflower, carrots and potatoes.

4. Simon got out of bed, dressed, came downstairs, ate his breakfast and went to school. 5. When did Sarah go shopping?
6. What a lovely dress!
7. The elephant's tusks and the bull's horns... weapons.
8. The books' pages... library.
9. you have 10. I have 11. shall not
12. are not 13. would've 14. hasn't
15. isn't 16. he'd
17. Royal Air Force
18. Her Majesty's Ship 19. Doctor
20. United Kingdom
21. Jenny shouted, "What's going on?"
22. "There's... here!" replied Sandra.
23. "If there's a ghost," stammered Dominic, "I'm off!"
24. "Who let the secret out?" demanded Don.
  "I don't know," replied Jack.
25. She... kitchen; she... supper; she... baby; she ... fire.
26. Follow these instructions: light... back.

Spelling

Test 26
1. Art English History Mathematics Science
2. black blue green orange red yellow
3. Friday Monday Saturday Sunday Thursday Tuesday Wednesday

4. thank then there these thing think those thought thud
5. saint sat saviour snake snarl sugar sweet swing switch

Test 27
(with suggested meaning)
1. bite   cut with your teeth
2. spine   backbone
3. cane   stick
4. mane   horse's hair
5. pane   window glass
6. kite   something to fly
7. pipe   tube
8. fate   destiny
9. pale   wan
10. wine   drink
11. twine string
12. made   created
13. note   short letter
14. fire   burning
15. mate   partner
16. spine
17. spin
18. sit
19. site
20. tap
21. tape
22. cut
23. cute

Test 28
earthquake
quarter queues
quickly questions
quench quoted
inquiry
pharaohs
philosophers
physicians
photographs
phenomenally
sphinx

Test 29
1. inn, hotel or pub
2. flour, milled grain
3. pail, bucket
4. knot, loop in

Answers

string
5. here, in this place
6. bear, animal
7. bread, food
8. tyre, rubber on wheel
9. tea, drink
10. hour, 60 minutes
11. heal, cure
12. beach
13. fare
14. meat
15. rode
16. would
17. heir, air
18. die, dye
19. ate, eight
20. buy, by
21. weak, week

Test 30
1. till
2. leaves
3. rulers
4. fast
5. left
6. bowl
7. c 8. d 9. b
10. e 11. a

Test 31
1. piece
2. field
3. deceive
4. thief
5. friend
6. relief
7. mischievous
8. shriek
9. shield
10. belief
11. patient
12. siege
13. chief
14. yield
15. rein
16. height
17. weight
18. sieve
19. achieve
20. view
21. diesel
22. grief
23. ceiling
24. eight
25. veil
26. sleigh
27. neighbour
28. priest
29. seize

30. protein
31. reign
32. frieze
33. alien
34. medieval
35. experience
36. series
37. tie
38. quiet
39. tier
40. perceive

Test 32
1. cabbage
2. lorry
3. below
4. desert
5. dessert
6. carrot
7. reddish
8. lettuce
9. different
10. hammer
11. completed
12. remained
13. foaming
14. cater
15. syllable
16. riding
17. dinner
18. supper
19. hatter
20. filling
21. filing
22. mopping
23. super
24. holly
25. miller
26. riper
27. Ripper
28. planing
29. bonniest
30. starring

Test 33
1. rectangular
2. dollar
3. fibber
4. doctor
5. farmer
6. behaviour
7. lawyer
8. cellar
9. meter/metre
10. triangular
11. pillar
12. helicopter
13. photographer
14. spectator
15. butcher

16. tractor
17. collar
18. lighter
19. humour
20. litter
21. sister
22. brother
23. centimetre
24. creator
25. slower
26. greater
27. editor
28. busier
29. vigour
30. character
31. particular
32. litre
33. matter
34. mother
35. glamour
36. assessor
37. donor
38. regular
39. murderer
40. viewer

Test 34
1. electrical
2. icicle
3. seasonal
4. knuckle
5. edible
6. cancel
7. reasonable
8. critical
9. article
10. particle
11. indecipherable
12. vehicle
13. fable
14. fictional
15. cubicle
16. physical
17. parcel
18. miracle
19. final
20. flammable
21. enjoyable
22. spherical
23. obstacle
24. mechanical
25. feeble
26. towel
27. thimble
28. saddle
29. total
30. inflatable
31. technical
32. horizontal
33. legal

34. ladle
35. lethal
36. level
37. travel
38. shovel
39. brutal
40. animal

Test 35
1. punctuation
2. electrician
3. association
4. exclamation
5. possession
6. position
7. session
8. section
9. sedition
10. politician
11. quotation
12. liberation
13. nation
14. tension
15. attention
16. confession
17. mansion
18. station
19. reception
20. mission
21. perdition
22. musician
23. moderation
24. physician
25. omission
26. occupation
27. obstruction
28. observation
29. passion
30. mathematician
31. petition
32. situation
33. meditation
34. prevention
35. deprivation
36. detention
37. qualification
38. concession
39. diversion
40. combination

Test 36
1. hog, horse, husky, hyena, mink, mongoose, monkey.
2. mad, crazy
3. fin, part of a fish
4. din, noise

5. aisle/isle
6. allowed/aloud
7. blew/blue
8. quay, quarter, quacking, quarrelling, quit.
9. Philip, hieroglyphics, pharmacist, phone, physics.
10. receive
11. pierce
12. either
13. friend
14. chief
15. conceited
16. accept
17. aided
18. taping
19. essential
20. fuming
21. error
22. supporter
23. meteor
24. metre/meter
25. flavour
26. victor
27. lunar
28. musical
29. muscle
30. legal
31. phenomenal
32. thimble
33. tumble
34. nation
35. deception
36. tension
37. negation
38. affirmation
39. decision